English in Focus: Works

ENGLISH IN FOCUS

English in Workshop Practice

ALAN MOUNTFORD

TEACHER'S EDITION

OXFORD UNIVERSITY PRESS

Oxford University Press, Walton Street, Oxford OX2 6DP

OXFORD LONDON GLASGOW
NEW YORK TORONTO MELBOURNE WELLINGTON
KUALA LUMPUR SINGAPORE JAKARTA HONG KONG TOKYO
DELHI BOMBAY CALCUTTA MADRAS KARACHI
IBADAN NAIROBI DAR ES SALAAM CAPE TOWN

ISBN 0 19 437511 0 (Students)

ISBN 0 19 437502 1 (Teachers)

First published 1975
Reprinted 1978

© Oxford University Press 1975

PRINTED AND BOUND IN ENGLAND BY
HAZELL WATSON AND VINEY LTD
AYLESBURY, BUCKS

Contents

Acknowledgements

I would like to thank John Southwell and J. S. Robertson for checking the manuscript from a technical point of view. I should also like to express my deep thanks to my wife for the hard work she has put into typing and preparing the final manuscript, and for her continual encouragement.

Several drawings are based on illustrations in *Part A* of *First Year Training for Engineering Craftsmen and Technicians*, by permission of the publishers, Engineering Industry Training Board, 54 Clarendon Road, Watford, Herts, from whom copies can be purchased at 80p each.

A. M.

Editors' Preface

The aim of the *English in Focus* series is to develop in students who are entering higher education an ability to handle the kind of written English that they will be concerned with as an integral part of their specialist subjects. The approach we have taken is one which recognizes that learning a language is not merely a matter of learning sentence patterns and vocabulary but must also involve an understanding of how people use these linguistic forms in order to communicate. Our purpose is to make students aware of the way English is used in actual written communication, and thereby to help them develop techniques of reading and to provide them with a guide for their own writing.

The books in this series are based on the belief that intermediate and advanced students who are studying English as a necessary part of their specialist studies need a distinctive type of textbook: one which reflects the nature of the learning problems actually encountered at this stage, and which presents the language as an aspect of the subject they are studying. We feel that a textbook directed at students at this level should attempt to do more than simply repeat the formulas in elementary language teaching material. Most courses of English concentrate on teaching the language system and fail to show how this system is used in communication. As a result, students may know about such formal items as affirmative sentences or modal verbs, but not know how these items are put to use in the making of different kinds of statement and in the production of continuous pieces of discourse.

The principal purpose of the *English in Focus* series is not to teach more grammar, but to show students how to use the grammar they already know. In writing these books two basic assumptions have been made. Firstly, it is assumed that the students have a good deal of instruction in grammar and that they have a considerable dormant competence in English. The books are directed at activating this competence, and extending it, by leading the reader to relate his previously acquired linguistic knowledge to meaningful realizations of the language system in passages of immediate relevance to his specialist studies. Secondly, it is assumed that the students already have a basic knowledge of their specialist subject. The aim is not to teach subject-matter but to develop in the reader an understanding of how this subject-matter is expressed through English. It should be emphasized that these books are not designed to teach either language in isolation or subject-matter in isolation but the manner in which both combine in meaningful communication. Our belief is that by relating content and expression in this way, the subject-matter takes on a new interest and the linguistic difficulties are reduced.

In order to ensure the natural communicative function of language we have graded by *focus* rather than by *exclusion*. Since we assume that the readers of these books already have a fairly wide knowledge of English grammar, and also have access to a standard dictionary and other reference books, the authors have been able to avoid an unnatural step-by-step presentation of grammatical patterns and vocabulary, and have instead tried to show how a fluent writer uses the whole resources of the language in performing various acts of communication. At the same time, care has been taken not to overload the student with new material and complex structures have been avoided except where they are necessary in maintaining a natural use of language. We believe that the books in the series will prepare the student to cope with greater linguistic complexity by developing in him a reading strategy which he can bring to bear on the material in the textbooks he has to read.

In the exercises we have attempted to avoid mechanical drills and repetitive pattern practice. The users of these books will be people whose minds are directed towards rational thought and problem-solving and the exercises have been designed to take this fact into account. Wherever possible, exercises are used which require the same kind of mental activity which students would naturally be engaged in as part of their specialist studies. It is hoped that this type of exercise will make the student see the relationship between expression and content, and will therefore persuade him of the relevance of English learning to his own specialist field. In the last resort, the authors depend on the student being prepared to teach himself, to concentrate diligently on the features of language exemplified in the texts, and to approach the linguistic content of these books with the same spirit of enquiry and desire for knowledge as he would be expected to bring to the study of his speciality.

It is appreciated that even in a series whose primary concern is with the written language, the teaching process must inevitably bring in the spoken form as well. Therefore, in order to assist both teacher and learner, the texts have been recorded, as also have those exercises containing additional vocabulary, the pronunciation of which might otherwise pose a problem.

J. P. B. A.
H. G. W.

Introduction

1. Guide to the book

This book consists of eight units. The first seven of these are each divided into two major sections:

I: Reading with comprehension problems, followed by exercises;
II: Grammar, followed by exercises.

Unit 8 has a different arrangement as the aim of this unit is to provide more reading passages which relate in language and content to the previous units. Section I of each of the seven units follows the same basic pattern. The basic pattern is as follows:

SECTION I
READING AND COMPREHENSION

The reading passage

Each section begins with a reading passage within which are inserted sets of comprehension checks in the form of statements which may or may not be correct. The learner has to decide on the correctness of each statement. These checks are inserted within the reading passage itself rather than at the end so as to encourage the learner to think about what he reads *as* he reads and to pay close attention to what is actually expressed in the passage. Once he realizes that his understanding is going to be systematically checked in this way he is likely to read more attentively for meaning and to treat his reading not simply as a language exercise relevant only to the English class but as a technique for acquiring information which will be useful in a wider field of study.

The comprehension checks require the learner to indicate whether a given statement is true or false according to the passage. But it is important that he should know *why* a statement is true or false and be able to recognize what it is in the passage that leads him to decide one way or the other. This is why each comprehension check is provided with a solution.

The Solutions

The solutions refer the learner to those features of the reading passage which provide evidence for the truth or falsehood of the statements in the comprehension checks. They are explanations in that they point out what the reader must notice and how he must reason in order to arrive at the correct decision. Explanations of this kind are of course not necessary for someone who already has an efficient reading ability in English. At first glance it might appear that the solutions are sometimes too elaborate and detailed. But it must be remembered that learners must be made aware of what is involved in reading with understanding before this ability can become habitual. The aim of these solutions is to develop in the learner a reading strategy which he can apply generally to the texts he has to deal with as part of his study of workshop practices.

Sometimes a solution will serve simply to remind the learner of the knowledge of English he already has. In Unit 1, for example comprehension check (a) requires the learner to recognize that two different words can refer to the same idea when they are joined together by a comma and 'or'. So, the solution appears simply as follows:

> One kind is called outside calipers. (4)
> They are used to measure outside, or external, diameters. (5)
>   x   y

x, or y, . . . i.e. y is another word for x

∴   outside diameters = external diameters

∴   *Outside calipers are used to measure external diameters.*

But the ability to recognize whether a given statement is true or not according to the passage does not only come from an understanding of the meaning of individual words and sentences. Very often it is a matter of recovering information which is implied rather than explicitly stated and of tracing the way in which what is expressed or implied in one sentence is related to what is expressed or implied in another. It is the function of many of the solutions, therefore, to make such implications explicit and to spell out the relationship between different statements.

Let us consider another example from Unit 1. In order to decide whether the statement 'All calipers have a stiff joint at the top of the legs' is true or not with reference to the passage (comprehension check (h), Unit 1) it is necessary to relate what is expressed in four different sentences: 13, 14, 16 and 17. This relating process is represented in the solution as follows (the symbols on the left indicate the kind of reasoning that is involved).

> The joint at the top of the legs acts as a hinge. (13)
> In some cases, this joint is stiff. (14)
> some ≠ (does not equal) all

∴ (*therefore*)   Not all calipers are of this stiff-jointed kind. (16)

i.e. (*that is to say*)   Not all calipers have stiff joints.

e.g. (*for example*)   Some calipers have a spring which joins the legs together. (17)

∴   It is NOT TRUE to say that all calipers have a stiff joint at the top of the legs.

What solutions of this kind do, then, is to spell out certain reasoning processes which are employed by the efficient reader as a matter of habit. Moreover, they are the sort of processes which are overtly employed in many fields of scientific and technological enquiry. Their use here as a language exercise is intended to appeal to the particular cognitive inclination of technical students, and to make them see that the content and the expression of technical writing are dependent upon each other.

The first three exercises following the reading passage* are a logical development from the solutions. Each focuses on a feature of language use which is frequently referred to in the solutions and which is particularly relevant to an understanding of how English is used in written communication.

EXERCISE A *Contextual reference*

This exercise draws the learner's attention to the way pronouns and demonstratives are used to refer to something already mentioned and so serve to relate one statement to another. Very often there is more than one *grammatically* possible connection between noun phrases and the reader has to decide which reference makes sense in the context of the passage concerned. This is the case, for example, with Exercise A 5 in Unit 1.

In sentence 11, *those* refers to:
(a) the points
(b) calipers
(c) the legs

Exercise A, then, obliges the learner to scrutinize the passage carefully to assign the correct referential 'value' to such 'anaphoric' language items as pronouns, demonstratives and so on. This exercise is not difficult, and it may sometimes seem obvious what a given item refers to. But again it must be remembered that we are not just concerned with getting the learner to recognize the contextual reference of a particular language item in a particular passage, but with developing a general ability to handle this feature of language use. The point is that this exercise directs the learner's attention to the way anaphoric devices work and so prepares him for those cases where identification of the referent is not so easy.

* Except Unit 2 where an exercise entitled 'Labelling a diagram' replaces 'Relationships between statements'.

EXERCISE B *Rephrasing*

Here again, the learner is made aware of how two different expressions may refer to the same thing. Whereas in Exercise A the problem is how to recognize that an expression like *those* refers to a previous noun phrase *the legs*, in this exercise the problem is to recognize that a phrase *curve away from each other* is synonymous with the phrase in the text *curve outwards* (see Exercise B 2, Unit 1). Essentially the purpose of this exercise is to make the learner realize that the same idea can be expressed in different ways and that there is no one-to-one correspondence between one linguistic form and one meaning. It is important that the students should realize this because two phrases may mean the same thing only within the context of a particular passage. For example, Exercise B 4 of Unit 1.

Spring calipers are opened and closed more easily than stiff-jointed calipers.

means the same as sentence 20 of Unit 1:

Calipers of this kind are more easily adjusted than the stiff-jointed kind.

We know this because sentence 19 makes use of the phrase *opened and closed* in discussing the legs of spring calipers. Sentence 20, in which *adjusted* occurs makes reference to sentence 19 by the phrase: *calipers of this kind*.

EXERCISE C *Relationships between statements (except Unit 2)*

Expressions like *therefore, consequently, however* etc. indicate what function a particular sentence is meant to fulfil. A sentence which contains *therefore* is used to make a statement which follows logically from a previous statement. Similarly, *for example* indicates that the sentence is used to make a statement which illustrates a point made previously. Such expressions are explicit indicators of the communicative function of sentences. But writers do not use explicit indicators in every sentence. Very often a writer assumes that the reader will realize how a particular sentence is to be understood without the assistance of such indicators. It is of course crucial for the student learning to read a foreign language to understand which statements are meant to be illustrations, qualifications, conclusions and so on, and how statements are logically related to each other. The purpose of this exercise then is to make the learner aware of such communicative functions and of the way written discourse develops.

Starting with Unit I, the learner is required to insert indicators in order to make explicit the relationship between sentences. For example, in Unit I the learner is given the following:

for this reason (7)
but (10+11)

Thus, the text after the insertion of these indicators will read:

[6]*The other kind is used to measure inside, or internal, diameters.* [7]*For this reason, they are known as inside calipers.*

[10]*The legs of outside calipers are curved and turn inwards at the points, but* [11]*those of inside calipers are straight and turn outwards at the points.*

Thus, sentence 6 is explicitly made a reason for naming a particular kind of calipers *inside calipers*, and the contrast between sentences 10 and 11 is made explicit by joining them with *but*.

Sometimes inserting such indicators involves making grammatical changes in the sentence. In Unit 3, for example, the learner is given the following:

may be classified (20)
we may compare . . . with . . . (28)

Sentence 20 of the reading passage is:

There are different types of hacksaw blade according to the number of teeth per inch.

This statement can be shown explicitly as introducing a classification which follows in the text by inserting the indicator as follows:

Hacksaw blades may be classified according to the number of teeth per inch.

Similarly, the comparison in sentence 28 can be rephrased as follows:

We may compare the cutting action of a file with that of a saw.

Sentence 29 describes in what particular way the file may be compared to the saw. The learner is then required to insert *therefore* in sentence 30, thus making it clear that sentence 30 is a deduction deriving from what has been stated previously.

Therefore, the file should be pressed down with both hands on the forward stroke.

The central purpose of this exercise, then, (notice *then*!) is to bring to the learner's notice the ways in which sentences are used to perform different acts of communication, and how such acts are related to one another in the development of a discourse.

Exercises A, B and C are designed to make little demand on the learner's productive ability. Their purpose is to direct the learner to a discovery of what is involved in the comprehension of written communication. The remaining exercises in each unit also involve comprehension but extend comprehension into written work.

THE REMAINING EXERCISES (D. E. F. etc)

These exercises vary in form from unit to unit but they have the same basic aim. This aim is to guide the learner to use his understanding of the reading passage to perform for himself the communicative acts which appear to be of particular importance in technical writing. Thus, in Unit I, the learner is required to manipulate information presented in a diagrammatic form in order to write definitions of common objects in terms of their use. In Unit 3 diagrams are used for producing definitions and generalizations, and in Unit 4 the learner is asked to construct diagrams to make classifications. In other units other acts of communication are presented in a similar way.

Two kinds of activity are given particular emphasis in these exercises. The first is what might be called *information transfer* and involves the use of written English to express facts and ideas presented in the form of diagrams. Technical students are, of course, familiar with the presentation of information in tables and worksheets with or without words. They are also familiar with the use of non-verbal means of communication like graphs, diagrams and line drawings. This activity of transferring information from a non-verbal to a verbal medium is intended to link the students' language learning with their main area of study. The second activity might be called *rhetorical transformation*. This involves changing one mode of communication into another. For example, in Unit 3 Exercise E, a definition like

A hacksaw is a tool which is used for cutting metal bars and strips.

can be changed, or transformed, into a generalization:

    A hacksaw is used for cutting metal bars and strips
or: *Hacksaws cut metal bars and strips.*

A more extreme example in Unit 3 occurs in Exercise F where information about different types of file is presented verbally in note form in a table. The object of the exercise is to transform these notes into descriptive statements. A further example may be taken from Unit 5 where the instructions for carrying out an operation together with the statement of its results can be transformed into inductive and deductive statements, or, as is shown in Unit 6, into descriptions.

Both information transfer and rhetorical transformation exercises are directed at showing the learner how he can use his knowledge of the formal properties of English to perform acts of communication which are characteristic of technical communication.

Three points should be noted finally. In addition to the types of exercise described above free use has been made of diagrams both as an aid, and a stimulus to comprehension. The exercises of Units 2 and 6 require the learner to comprehend language in relation to accompanying diagrams. There are also diagram labelling exercises in Units 1, 2, 7, and 8. Secondly, the topic of the reading passage for each unit is the source of much of the content of the exercises. Thus the content of the exercises of Units 1 and 2, entitled 'Calipers' and 'The micrometer' is mainly concerned with workshop tools and instruments. The exercises of Unit 3 relate to the topic of the reading passage, 'Bench work', while simple forge operations are used to exemplify inductions and deductions in Unit 5. Thirdly, it should be noted that many of the exercises are divided into several parts. This has been done in order to exploit the same material in different ways. In Unit 1, Exercise E, for example, Part 1 is concerned simply with establishing the formal pattern of a definition. Part 2 introduces other items to be defined by matching two lists. Part 3 introduces alternative forms of the definitions already made. Exercise F Part 1 then rhetorically transforms definitions into simple statements of use, using the information from Exercise E, and Part 2 of Exercise F introduces statements of composition, which may also be incorporated into definitions, to be taken up in Unit 2.

SECTION II
GRAMMAR

As stated above, it is assumed that the student already has a knowledge of basic grammar. It is also assumed that this knowledge will be consolidated during the course of the book as the student experiences language used in meaningful contexts. For these reasons no attempt has been made to provide a detailed review of English grammar. Instead, the exercises in this section are designed to focus on points of grammar which are particularly important in technical writing, especially those which may represent continuing trouble spots for many students.

In designing the exercises an attempt has been made to present grammar in the context of discourse. Thus, in Unit 2, the exercise on the passive is basically a conversion exercise familiar to most teachers. However, by setting the forms to be converted from active to passive in connected sentences, some of which may be joined by conjunctions such as *when* and *because*, the lack of communicative purpose in conventional single sentence conversion exercises has been avoided. Again with the exercises on expressions of purpose, reason etc. in Unit 3, the approach emphasizes the meaning of the relationship between two sentences as much as the formal manipulation of *to-infinitives* or expressions like *in order to* or *so that*. The same approach characterizes the exercises on time expressions in Unit 6 and modal verbs in Unit 7. As with the exercises in Section I the unit topic has guided the content of many of the grammar exercises.

2. Teaching suggestions

The following notes indicate how the first unit might be dealt with in the classroom. The other units can be handled in a similar way. These notes are intended to be suggestions only. It is expected that the teacher will develop his own procedures according to the needs and abilities of his students. A particular teacher, for example, may find that he needs to place greater emphasis on one type of exercise than on another. He may wish to pay more attention to oral than to written work, or the reverse. It will also be up to the teacher to decide, according to his own circumstances, how the work is to be divided into class sections, and which part of it can be most appropriately done as homework.

I   READING AND COMPREHENSION

(i) Reading the text

Get the class to read sentences 1–7 by themselves.

Take the class through the explanation so that it is clear what they have to do.

Get the class to do comprehension question (c) on their own.

Choose one student. Ask him whether he has answered 'true' or 'not true' for question (c). Get him to justify his decision with reference to the appropriate parts of the text. Ask other students whether they agree and if not why not. Get the class to turn to the relevant solution. Read it aloud to the class while the students follow it in their books.

Read sentences 1–7 aloud to the class, while they follow in their books.

Get the class to read sentences 8–12 by themselves.

Get the class to do questions (d)–(f) on their own, and repeat the process as for question (c).

Read the whole passage aloud to the class, without the questions while the students follow in their books.

(ii) Exercises

EXERCISE A *Contextual reference*

Get the class to do the exercise in their notebooks.

Ask the class to show which choices they have made in question 1 by putting up their hands.

Ask students to replace the item in italics with the phrase they have chosen, and read out the sentence which results. For example, a student choosing 1(a) will read out *Objects can be used to measure diameters of metal bars or tubes* and a student choosing 1(b) will read out *Calipers can be used to measure diameters of metal bars or tubes.*

Ask the class to judge which is correct.

Repeat the process for questions 2–6.

EXERCISE B *Rephrasing*

Get the class to do the exercise in their notebooks.

When the class has finished the exercise, write the first sentence on the board. Underline the expression which is to be replaced.

Select a volunteer to come to the board and write in the replacing expression above the words which are underlined.

Ask the class to judge whether the rephrasing is appropriate. Consider alternatives if necessary.

Bracket together the appropriate replacement(s) with the original expression as follows:

Outside calipers can be used to measure the

$\begin{Bmatrix} \textit{distance across the outside} \\ \textit{diameter} \end{Bmatrix}$ *of a metal bar.*

Do the remaining sentences in the same way.

EXERCISE C *Relationships between statements*

Take the class through the explanation so they know what to do.
Get the class to do the exercise in their notebooks.
When the class have finished the exercise write sentences 6 and 7 on the board.
Ask a student to read out the two sentences with the expression *for this reason* inserted in the correct place in sentence 7.
Modify sentence 7 on the board accordingly. Thus:

> *The other kind is used to measure inside or internal diameters. They are known as inside calipers*

will become

> *The other kind is used to measure inside or internal diameters. For this reason they are known as inside calipers.*

Do the remaining sentences.
When finished ask a student to read out the text with the indicators inserted and appropriate changes made.

EXERCISE D *Labelling of diagrams*

Get the class to label the diagrams in their notebooks.
Check their answers orally.

EXERCISE E *The definition of objects in terms of class and use*

Part 1

Take the class through the explanation so they know what to do.
Ask individual students to compose definitions orally according to the example using the information in the boxes.
After completing the exercise orally, get students to write out the definitions in their notebooks.

Part 2

Get the students to read the two lists carefully with reference to the diagrams.
Ask a student to identify the objects in (a). Ask him what they are used for.

Ask him whether they are instruments or tools. Get him to define the objects using this information.
Do the remaining objects and get students to write out the definitions in their notebooks.

Part 3

Ask students to write out the alternative forms of definitions in their notebooks. This can be done for homework and checked orally in class afterwards.

EXERCISE F *General statements*

Parts 1 and 2

Get the students to do the exercise in their notebooks. Check orally.
or:

Go through half the exercise orally in class and then ask students to complete it in their notebooks.

II GRAMMAR
EXERCISE A

Get the students to read the grammatical explanation carefully.
Allow them several minutes to study the three columns. Do three of the definitions orally in each of the five patterns.
Get the students to write these and the rest of the exercise in their notebooks.
Go round the class and give individual help when necessary.
Check orally when completed.

EXERCISES B and C

Get the students to study the examples carefully.
Do the first three orally using the patterns given in the examples.
Get the students to write these and the rest of the exercise in their notebooks.
Check orally when completed.

1 Calipers

I READING AND COMPREHENSION

¹Calipers are instruments which are used for measuring the dimensions of small objects. ²They can be used to measure diameters of metal bars or tubes. ³There are two kinds of calipers. ⁴One kind is called outside calipers. ⁵They are used to measure outside, or external, diameters. ⁶The other kind is used to measure inside, or internal, diameters. ⁷They are known as inside calipers.

Study the following statements carefully and write down whether they are true or not true, according to the information expressed in sentences 1–7 above. Then check your answers by referring to the solutions at the end of the passage.*

(a) Outside calipers are used to measure external diameters.
(b) External calipers can be used to measure the external dimensions of any metal object.
(c) Calipers can be used to measure the diameters of metal tubes.

⁸Both kinds consist of two pieces of metal which are joined together at the top. ⁹They are called legs and are pointed at the ends. ¹⁰The legs of outside calipers are curved and turn inwards at the points. ¹¹Those of inside calipers are straight and turn outwards at the points. ¹²Measurements are taken between the points and are read off on a rule.

(d) Caliper legs are pointed at the ends.
(e) Inside calipers have straight legs.
(f) The legs of outside calipers point inwards at the ends.

   * The following symbols are used in the solutions:
i.e. that is to say
e.g. for example
= equals/means the same as
≠ does not equal/does not mean the same as
∴ therefore

[13]The joint at the top of the legs acts as a hinge. [14]In some cases this joint is stiff. [15]The legs are kept open by means of friction. [16]Not all calipers are of this stiff-jointed kind. [17]Some calipers have a spring which joins the legs together. [18]They are known as spring calipers. [19]The legs are opened and closed by turning a nut on a screw. [20]Calipers of this kind are more easily adjusted than the stiff-jointed kind.

(g) Spring calipers are opened by turning a nut on a screw.
(h) All calipers have a stiff joint at the top of the legs.
(i) The legs of spring calipers are kept open by means of friction.
(j) Spring calipers are easier to adjust than stiff-jointed calipers.

Solutions

(a) One kind is called outside calipers. (4)
    They are used to measure [**X** outside], or [**Y** external], diameters. (5)
    X, or **Y**, . . . i.e. **Y** is another word for **X**.
∴ outside diameters = external diameters
∴ *Outside calipers are used to measure external diameters.*

(b) Calipers are instruments which are used for measuring the dimensions of small objects. (1)
    small objects ≠ any objects
∴ It is NOT TRUE to say that external calipers can be used to measure the external dimensions of any metal object.

(c) They (i.e. calipers) can be used to measure diameters of metal bars or tubes. (2)
    metal bars or tubes = both metal bars and metal tubes (cf. (a))
∴ *Calipers can be used to measure diameters* (=*the diameters*) *of metal tubes.*

(d) . . . two strips of metal are joined together at the top. (8)
    They are called legs . . . (9)
i.e. Caliper legs are joined together at the top.
    . . . and are pointed at the ends. (9)
i.e. *Caliper legs are pointed at the ends.*

(e) Those (i.e. the legs) of inside calipers are straight. (11)
= *Inside calipers have straight legs.*

(f) The legs of outside calipers are curved and turn inwards at the points. (10)
i.e. The legs of outside calipers turn inwards at the points.
    turn inwards at the points = point inwards at the ends (see (d))
i.e. *The legs of outside calipers point inwards at the ends.*

(g) They are known as spring calipers. (18)
   The legs are opened and closed by turning a nut on a screw. (19)
i.e. The legs of spring calipers are opened . . . by turning a nut on a screw.
  = *Spring calipers are opened by turning a nut on a screw.*

(h) The joint at the top of the legs acts as a hinge. (13)
   In some cases this joint is stiff. (14)
   some $\neq$ all
  ∴ Not all calipers are of this stiff-jointed kind. (16)
i.e. Not all calipers have stiff joints.
e.g. Some calipers have a spring which joins the legs together. (17)
  ∴ It is NOT TRUE to say that all calipers have a stiff joint at the top of the legs.

(i) The legs are kept open by means of friction. (15)
i.e. The legs of stiff-jointed calipers (16) are kept open by means of friction.
   The legs of spring calipers (18) are opened or closed by turning a nut on a screw. (19)
  ∴ The legs of spring calipers are NOT kept open by means of friction.

(j) Calipers of this kind (i.e. spring calipers (18)) are more easily adjusted than the stiff-jointed kind. (20)
   are more easily adjusted = are easier to adjust
i.e. *Spring calipers are easier to adjust than stiff-jointed calipers.*

EXERCISE A *Contextual reference*

1. In sentence 2, *they* refers to:
   (a) objects
   (b) calipers
   (c) dimensions

2. In sentence 5, *they* refers to:
   (a) two kinds
   (b) outside calipers
   (c) calipers

3. In sentence 7, *they* refers to:
   (a) calipers which measure internal diameters
   (b) calipers which measure external diameters

4. In sentence 9, *they* refers to:
   (a) both kinds
   (b) the ends
   (c) two pieces of metal

5. In sentence 11, *those* refers to:
    (a) the points
    (b) calipers
    (c) the legs

6. In sentence 18, *they* refers to:
    (a) calipers which have a spring
    (b) the legs
    (c) all calipers

EXERCISE B *Rephrasing*

Compare these sentences:

(i) Outside calipers can be used to measure the *distance* between *the outsides* of a metal bar.

(ii) Outside calipers can be used to measure the external diameter of a metal bar.

These two sentences mean the same thing. The second sentence contains an alternative form used in the text. Now re-write the following, using words and constructions from the text to replace those printed in italics.

1. *The length and width* of a small metal object can be measured by using calipers.
2. The legs of inside calipers curve *away from each other* at the points.
3. Some calipers have a spring which joins the legs together, but others *have a joint at the top of the legs which is stiff.*
4. Spring calipers are *opened and closed* more easily than stiff-jointed calipers.

EXERCISE C *Relationships between statements*

In this book you will meet many words and phrases which can be used to connect statements. Two of the most common are:

(i) for example   (ii) because

Look at the following:

(i)   [a] Calipers are instruments which are used for measuring the dimensions of small objects. (1)
         [b] They can be used to measure diameters. (2)
    [a+b] Calipers are instruments which are used for measuring the dimensions of small objects. *For example*, they can be used to measure diameters.

(ii)   [a] One kind is called outside calipers. (4)
         [b] They are used to measure outside, or external, diameters. (5)
    [a+b] One kind is called outside calipers *because* they are used to measure outside, or external, diameters.

In (i), statement [b] gives an example of statement [a].

In (ii), statement [b] gives the reason why statement [a] is true.

Now place the following words or phrases in the sentences indicated:

(a) for this reason (7)

(b) but (10+11)

(c) as a result (15)

(d) however (16)

(e) for example (17)

(f) therefore (18)

(g) consequently (20)

EXERCISE D *Labelling of diagrams*

Write down the names of the calipers illustrated below and of the parts indicated.

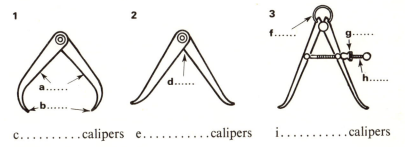

c..........calipers   e...........calipers   i..........calipers

EXERCISE E *The definition of objects in terms of class and use*

Part 1

We can define an object by saying

(a) what *class* of objects it belongs to, and

(b) what we *use* it for.

EXAMPLES

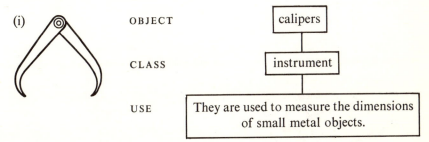

OBJECT	calipers
CLASS	instrument
USE	They are used to measure the dimensions of small metal objects.

DEFINITION

Calipers *are* instruments *which* are used to measure the dimensions of small metal objects.

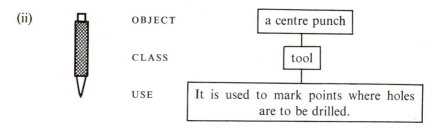

(ii)   OBJECT   a centre punch

CLASS   tool

USE   It is used to mark points where holes are to be drilled.

DEFINITION

A centre punch *is a* tool *which* is used to mark points where holes are to be drilled.

Below are illustrations of common objects. Using the information in the boxes, write out complete definitions of each object as in the examples above.

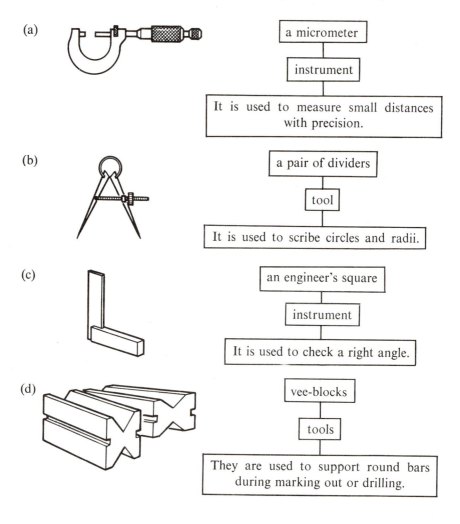

(a)   a micrometer

instrument

It is used to measure small distances with precision.

(b)   a pair of dividers

tool

It is used to scribe circles and radii.

(c)   an engineer's square

instrument

It is used to check a right angle.

(d)   vee-blocks

tools

They are used to support round bars during marking out or drilling.

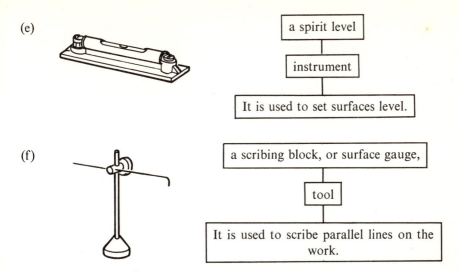

(e)

a spirit level

instrument

It is used to set surfaces level.

(f)

a scribing block, or surface gauge,

tool

It is used to scribe parallel lines on the work.

Part 2

Look at the illustrations (a)–(f). Following the illustrations there are two lists, A and B.
Write a definition of each object, using a name from list A and a sentence from list B.
In your definitions, say whether the object is an *instrument* or a *tool*.

EXAMPLE:
    A scriber is a tool which is used to mark lines on metal.

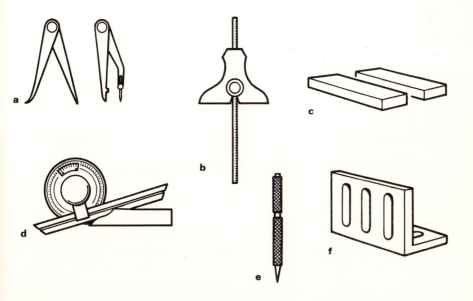

a

b

c

d

e

f

List A: parallel strips   a depth gauge
           a scriber   a vernier protractor
           an angle plate   odd-leg calipers

List B: They are used to scribe lines which are parallel to an edge.
           It is used to support a surface at right angles to the marking-out
           table.
           It is used to measure angles.
           It is used to measure depths.
           It is used to mark lines on metal.
           They are used to support work on the marking-out table.

Part 3

We can write the definitions from Parts 1 and 2 in other ways.

EXAMPLES

(i) Calipers are instruments which are used to measure the dimensions
of small metal objects.

OR (ii) Calipers are instruments which are used *for* measur*ing* the dimensions
of small metal objects.

OR (iii) Calipers are instruments which *measure* the dimensions of small
metal objects.

Write out the definitions which you have made in Parts 1 and 2 above, as in
examples (ii) and (iii).

EXERCISE F *General statements*

Part 1

We can make *general statements* about different objects by naming them and
saying what they are used for but without saying what class they belong to.

EXAMPLE

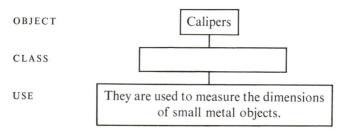

OBJECT   CLASS   USE

GENERAL STATEMENT

Calipers are used to measure the dimensions of small metal objects.
OR: Calipers are used *for* measur*ing* the dimensions of small metal
objects.

Make statements about the following tools and instruments using the information from Exercise E, Parts 1 and 2 above.

(a) a micrometer
(b) a scribing block
(c) an angle plate
(d) an engineer's square

(e) a spirit level
(f) vee-blocks
(g) parallel strips
(h) a scriber

(i) a vernier protractor
(f) a depth gauge

Part 2

We can make statements about different objects by naming them and saying what they are made of.

EXAMPLE
Calipers . . . . . . hardened steel.
Calipers are made of hardened steel.

Make statements about the following tools and instruments. Say what they are made of by choosing an appropriate expression from the list on the right.

(a) an engineer's rule
(b) the blade of a try-square
(c) a surface table
(d) vee-blocks
(e) the stock of a try-square
(f) scribers
(g) a toolmaker's clamp
(h) centre punches
(i) files

mild steel
hardwood
cast iron
tool steel
high carbon steel
silver steel
case-hardened steel

II GRAMMAR

EXERCISE A *Forms of definitions*

Study the following patterns

1. [A A vernier height gauge] is [B an instrument] which [C is used for measuring heights very accurately].
2. [A A vernier height gauge] may be defined as [B an instrument] which [C is used for measuring heights very accurately].
3. One may define [A a vernier height gauge] as [B an instrument] which [C is used for measuring heights very accurately].
4. [B An instrument] which [C is used for measuring heights very accurately] is called [A a vernier height gauge].
5. [B An instrument] which [C is used for measuring heights very accurately] is known as [A a vernier height gauge].

We may state the patterns as follows:

1. [A] is/are [B] which [C].
2. [A] may be defined as [B] which [C].
3. One may define [A] as [B] which [C].
4. [B] which [C] is/are called [A].
5. [B] which [C] is/are known as [A].

Expand the following into full definitions. Write each definition five times, *i.e.* in each of the patterns given above.

[A]	[B]	[C]
1. A die	a tool	is used for cutting an external thread.
2. Templates	patterns	are used for the fast marking out of difficult shapes.
3. A lathe	a machine	is used to turn and cut metal.
4. Plug gauges	instruments	are used for checking hole diameters.
5. Soldering	a process	joins metal to metal using a fusible alloy.
6. Silver steel	a ferrous metal	contains 98% iron, 1% carbon and 0·5% chromium.
7. Conductivity	the property	enables a metal to conduct heat or electricity easily.
8. A machine tool	a power-driven machine	is designed to hold a workpiece and cutting tool and produce a finished surface.

EXERCISE B *The use of nouns and adjectives in definitions* (*Shapes*)

EXAMPLE

x is a *circle*

y is a *wheel*

y is an object in the shape of x.

i.e. (i) A wheel is an object *in the shape of a circle*.
OR (ii) A wheel is an object *of circular shape*.
OR (iii) A wheel is a *circular* object.

Note: *A wheel is a circular object* ... is the first part of a definition:
NAME OF OBJECT+CLASS ... (See Exercise E, Part 1)

Make three statements about each of the following objects using the patterns given above.

(a) 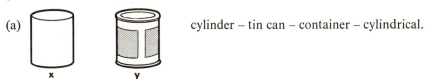 cylinder – tin can – container – cylindrical.

(b) 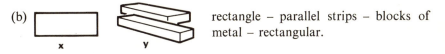 rectangle – parallel strips – blocks of metal – rectangular.

(c) 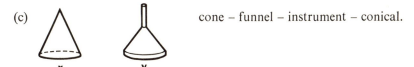 cone – funnel – instrument – conical.

(d) 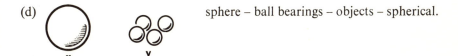 sphere – ball bearings – objects – spherical.

(e) 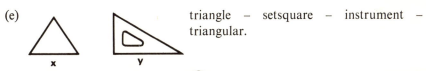 triangle – setsquare – instrument – triangular.

(f)  rectangle – straight edge – strip of steel – rectangular.

EXERCISE C *The use of nouns and adjectives in general statements* (*Dimensions*)

1. Write four statements about the dimensions of each of the objects illustrated below using the expressions given in the example.

EXAMPLE  metal bar – long – length

(i) The metal bar is 100 mm *long*. (100 mm = a hundred millimetres)

OR (ii) The *length* of the metal bar is 100 mm.

OR (iii) The metal bar *has a length of* 100 mm.

OR (iv) The metal bar is 100 mm *in length*.

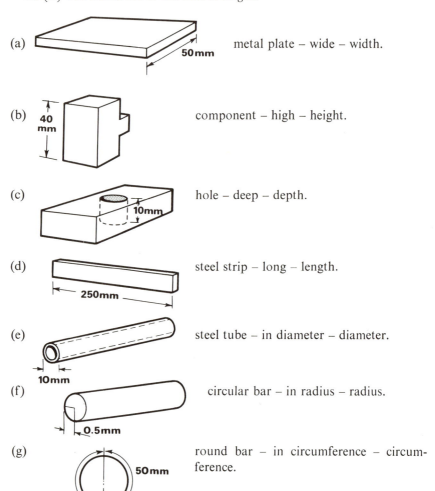

(a)   50 mm   metal plate – wide – width.

(b)   40 mm   component – high – height.

(c)   10 mm   hole – deep – depth.

(d)   250 mm   steel strip – long – length.

(e)   10 mm   steel tube – in diameter – diameter.

(f)   0.5 mm   circular bar – in radius – radius.

(g)   50 mm   round bar – in circumference – circumference.

2. State the dimensions of the objects (a)–(f) illustrated below, as in the examples (i–iv).

EXAMPLES

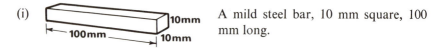

(i)   10 mm   100 mm   10 mm   A mild steel bar, 10 mm square, 100 mm long.

(ii) A bar, of 15 mm diameter, 50 mm long.

(iii) A block of metal, 17 mm by 15 mm by 35 mm long.

(iv) A mild steel plate, 5 mm thick.

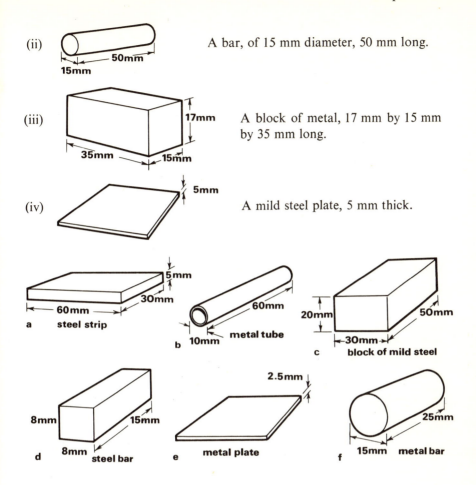

a   steel strip

b   metal tube

c   block of mild steel

d   steel bar

e   metal plate

f   metal bar

2 The micrometer

I READING AND COMPREHENSION

Read this passage and deal with the comprehension problems as in Unit 1.

[1]A micrometer is an instrument which is used for measuring small distances precisely. [2]It can measure with a precision of 0·01 mm. [3]A micrometer consists of a steel frame in the shape of a semi-circle. [4]Attached to one end of this semi-circular frame is a small anvil. [5]The other end of the frame extends outwards. [6]A piece of metal in the shape of a cylinder fits on to this extension. [7]This cylindrical part is called the barrel, or sleeve.

(a) The barrel is a cylindrical piece of metal which fits on to an extension of the frame.
(b) A micrometer is a precision instrument.

[8]Inside the barrel is a screw thread. [9]A spindle screws through the barrel. [10]Connected to the spindle is another cylindrical piece of metal called the thimble which fits over the barrel. [11]Attached to the end of the thimble is a ratchet, which turns the spindle. [12]Most micrometers have a lock nut, or locking ring, so that the spindle can be locked in any position. [13]Measurements are taken between the anvil and the end of the spindle. [14]They are read off from numbers which are marked on the barrel and on the thimble.

(c) The thimble is attached to the spindle.
(d) There is a screw thread inside the barrel.
(e) Micrometers always have a lock nut to lock the spindle in any position.
(f) The spindle is turned by a ratchet on the end of the thimble.

[15]A micrometer works like a screw which is turned in a nut which is fixed. [16]If a screw is turned once in a stationary nut, it will move forward a small distance. [17]This distance is equal to the pitch of the thread of the nut. [18]Let us say that the screw thread of the barrel of a micrometer is 0·025″ in pitch. [19]If the spindle is rotated one revolution, it will move forward a distance of 0·025″

(g) A micrometer works like a screw which is turned in a stationary nut.

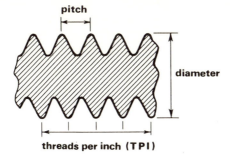

Solutions

(a) The other end of the frame extends outwards. (5)
A piece of metal in the shape of a cylinder fits on to this extension. (6)
This cylindrical part is called the barrel. (7)
∴ *The barrel is a cylindrical piece of metal which fits on to an extension of the frame.*

(b) A micrometer is an instrument which is used for measuring small distances precisely. (1)
It can measure with a precision of 0·01 mm. (2)
∴ *A micrometer is a precision instrument.*

(c) connected to (10) = attached to (11)
Connected to the spindle is another cylindrical piece of metal called the thimble . . . (10)
= Another cylindrical piece of metal called the thimble is attached to the spindle.
i.e. *The thimble is attached to the spindle.*

(d) Inside the barrel is a screw thread. (8)
= Inside the barrel there is a screw thread.
= *There is a screw thread inside the barrel.*

(e) Most micrometers have a lock nut . . . (12)
i.e. Not all micrometers have a lock nut.
i.e. Micrometers DO NOT always have a lock nut to lock the spindle in any position.

(f) Attached to the end of the thimble is a ratchet, which turns the spindle. (11)
i.e. [X A ratchet] turns [Y the spindle].

=   [Y The spindle] is turned by [**X** a ratchet].
    attached to the end of the thimble = on the end of the thimble
i.e. *The spindle is turned by a ratchet on the end of the thimble.*

(g) A micrometer works like a screw which is turned in a nut which is fixed.
    (15)
    a nut which is fixed = a stationary nut (16)
∴   *A micrometer works like a screw which is turned in a stationary nut.*

EXERCISE A *Contextual reference*

1. In sentence 2 *it* refers to:
   (a) any instrument
   (b) a micrometer
   (c) a small distance
2. In sentence 14, *they* refers to:
   (a) the anvil and the end of the spindle
   (b) measurements
3. In sentence 16, *it* refers to:
   (a) a nut
   (b) a screw
   (c) a micrometer
4. In sentence 19, *it* refers to:
   (a) the barrel
   (b) the screw thread
   (c) the spindle

EXERCISE B *Rephrasing*

Rewrite the following, using words and constructions from the text to replace those printed in italics. For examples, see Unit 1, Exercise B, Rephrasing.

1. A micrometer can measure *differences between dimensions which are as small as* 0·01 mm.
2. There is a small anvil inside one end of the *frame which is in the shape of a semi-circle.*
3. A spindle screws through the *cylindrical part which is attached to the frame.*
4. The spindle is locked in position by a *lock nut.*
5. If the spindle of a micrometer is *turned* one *complete circle*, the distance that it will move forward is equal to the pitch of the *thread of the screw* of the barrel.

EXERCISE C *Labelling a diagram*

Write down the names of the parts of the micrometer indicated by the arrows.

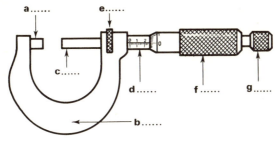

EXERCISE D *Description of a micrometer through the selection of words from alternatives*

Write a description of a micrometer by choosing the correct expressions from the alternatives given below.

A micrometer consists of a [CYLINDRICAL/RECTANGULAR/SEMI-CIRCULAR] steel [ANVIL/FRAME/BARREL]. Inside one end is a small [ANVIL/RATCHET/LOCK NUT]. Attached to an extension of the other end of the [FRAME/SPINDLE/BARREL] is a [SEMI-CIRCULAR/CYLINDRICAL/TRIANGULAR] [BARREL/THIMBLE/SPINDLE], or sleeve. A [THIMBLE/SPINDLE/LOCK NUT] screws through the barrel.
Connected to the spindle is the [THIMBLE/SLEEVE/RATCHET] to the end of which is attached a [LOCKING RING/RATCHET/ANVIL] which turns the spindle. The spindle can be locked in any position by a [LOCK NUT/RATCHET/SCREW].
Measurements are [TAKEN/READ OFF] between the [ANVIL AND THE BARREL/SPINDLE AND THE THIMBLE/SPINDLE AND THE ANVIL] and are [TAKEN/READ OFF] from numbers marked on the barrel and thimble.

EXERCISE E *Description of objects in terms of their main parts and construction*

Part 1

Make statements about the position of A in relation to B in the following diagrams by using the given expressions.

EXAMPLES

(i) [A   B]   end

     A is attached *to the end* of B.
OR A is attached to B *at the end.*

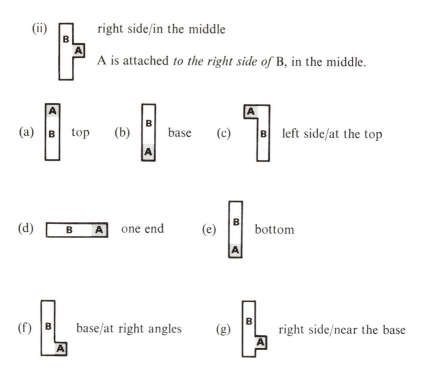

(ii)   right side/in the middle

A is attached *to the right side of* B, in the middle.

(a)   top   (b)   base   (c)   left side/at the top

(d)   one end   (e)   bottom

(f)   base/at right angles   (g)   right side/near the base

Part 2

Make statements about how the following parts of common hand tools and instruments are joined by using the given expressions.

EXAMPLES

(i) anvil : micrometer : attached : one end : frame :
The anvil of a micrometer is attached to one end of the frame.

(ii) barrel : micrometer : joined : frame : other end :
The barrel of a micrometer is joined to the frame at the other end.

(a) wing nut : hacksaw : attach : forward end : frame :
(b) ratchet : micrometer : attach : one end : thimble :
(c) legs : calipers : riveted : each other : top :
(d) blade : engineer's square : set into : one end : stock : right angles : frame :
(e) clamps : hacksaw : connected : bottom : handle: and : end : frame :
(f) legs : dividers : connected : each other : top : with a spring :
(g) handle : file : fits on to : pointed end : body, known as the tang :
(h) shaft : hammer : fits on to : head : right angles :
(i) scriber : scribing block : fixed : side : vertical spindle :
(j) adjusting screw : surface gauge : attach : one end : rocker arm :

Part 3

Study this example.

EXAMPLE

 one end/pointed

One end of A is pointed.
A has a pointed end.

Now make statements about the part of each object A below which is indicated by the arrow.

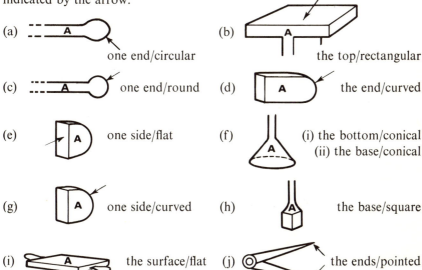

(a) one end/circular

(b) the top/rectangular

(c) one end/round

(d) the end/curved

(e) one side/flat

(f) (i) the bottom/conical
(ii) the base/conical

(g) one side/curved

(h) the base/square

(i) the surface/flat

(j) the ends/pointed

Note that we can also say:
A is pointed *at* one end.
A is curved *at* the end.
A is pointed *at* the ends.
etc.

EXERCISE F *Re-ordering of sentences to build descriptive paragraphs*

Below are illustrations of common tools and instruments. The sentences describe the main parts of these objects.
1. Rewrite the sentences in the order indicated by the letters (a, b, c etc.) which point to those parts.
   Write the sentences as a continuous short paragraph.
2. Change the words printed in italics in the following way:
   (i) change *nouns* to *pronouns*.
   (ii) change *indefinite articles* to *definite articles*.
   (iii) leave out phrases which are not necessary.

EXAMPLE
The legs are joined together at the top by a rivet.

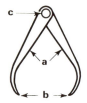

Outside calipers consist of two curved pieces of metal known as legs.

The legs are pointed at the ends.

a. Outside calipers consist of two curved pieces of metal known as legs.
b. The legs are pointed at the ends. c. *The legs* are joined together at the top by a rivet.

=   Outside callipers consist of two curved pieces of metal known as legs. The legs are pointed at the ends. They are joined together at the top by a rivet.

1. *A* blade is set into *a* stock at right angles. A brass strip may protect the face of the stock.
A try square consists of a blade and a stock.
The blade is held by steel pins.

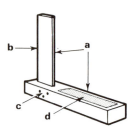

2. *The two legs* are connected part way down by a screw.
Engineers' dividers consist of two flat strips of metal which are known as legs.
There is a spring at the top of the legs which keeps *the legs* open.
The legs have pointed ends.
A nut on *a* screw adjusts the setting *of the legs*.

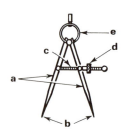

3. The other side *of the head* is curved and known as the pein.
The shaft is secured with wedges.
A ball-pein hammer consists of a head and a shaft.
One side of the head is flat and called the striking face.
A shaft fits into the head at right angles.

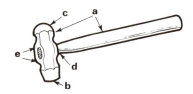

4. *The tang* fits into the handle.
A hand file consists of a rectangular body.
The end of the handle is protected by a ferrule.
One end *of the body* is pointed. This *pointed end* is called the tang.
The body is cut diagonally by grooves.

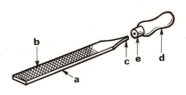

5. *A* blade is put in the frame with the teeth pointing away from the handle.
Clamps are connected to the bottom of the handle and the end of the frame.
A hacksaw consists of a frame.
A wing nut which is attached to the forward end of the frame adjusts the tightness of the blade.
The frame is curved at one end.
Attached to the other end *of the frame* is a handle.

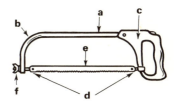

EXERCISE G *Definitions plus descriptions of objects*

A fuller description of the objects in Exercise F could begin with a definition and might include an expression saying what the object is made from. (see the reading text, sentences 1–14)

Re-order the following groups of sentences so as to make continuous paragraphs which describe the objects. Change the words printed in italics as you did in Exercise F. Always begin the description with a definition.

EXAMPLE

The legs turn inwards and are pointed at the ends.
The pieces of metal are made from hardened steel.
Outside calipers are instruments which are used for measuring the external dimensions of round metal objects.
The legs are riveted together at the top to form a stiff joint.
Outside calipers consist of two curved pieces of metal which are known as legs.

= Outside calipers are instruments which are used for measuring the external dimensions of round metal objects. *They* consist of two curved pieces of metal which are known as legs. *They* are made from hardened steel. The legs turn inwards and are pointed at the ends. *They* are riveted together at the top to form a stiff joint.

1. *A* blade *of a try-square* is set into the stock at right angles.
   A brass strip protects the face of the stock.
   A try-square is an instrument which is used for checking a right angle.
   A blade *of a try-square* is made of mild steel, and *a* stock *of a try-square* is made of hardwood.
   The blade is held by steel pins.
   A try-square consists of a blade and a stock.

2. A nut on *a* screw adjusts the setting of the legs.
   Dividers consist of two flat strips of metal known as legs.
   Engineers' dividers are tools which are used for scribing circles and marking off lengths and arcs.
   The strips of metal are made of hardened steel.
   There is a spring at the top of the legs which keeps *the legs* open.
   The two legs are connected half way down by a screw.

3. The pointed end of the body is called the tang.
   One end of the handle is protected by a ferrule.
   A hand file is a tool which is used for cutting metal.
   The body is cut diagonally by grooves.
   A hand file consists of a rectangular body which is made of hardened steel.
   The tang fits into the handle.

4. Add definitions to the descriptions of a *ball-pein hammer* and *a hacksaw* in Exercise F above, and make all the necessary changes.

II GRAMMAR:

THE PASSIVE

The impersonal passive is very common in technical writing. It is used for *describing procedures* and *stating rules*. Look at the following active and passive sentences and note that passive sentences contain some form of the verb *to be* together with a past participle.

ACTIVE	PASSIVE
We prepare a surface.	A surface *is* prepar*ed*.
We mark out a surface.	A surface *is* mark*ed* out.
We can use dividers to scribe circles.	Dividers can *be* use*d* to scribe circles.
We brushed the surfaces with a marking-out medium.	The surfaces *were* brushed with a marking-out medium.

Notice that the passive sentences bring into a prominent position the thing to which an action is done by placing it at the beginning of the sentence.

ACTIVE	PASSIVE
A blow torch heats the metal bar to dull red.	A metal bar is heated to dull red (by a blow torch.)

The words in brackets are often omitted in technical writing.
Write down the passive version of the active sentences given below. Then complete the combined sentences underneath, by providing words for the blank spaces. First, study the example carefully.

EXAMPLE
   Active: A screw controls spring calipers.
   Passive: Spring calipers *are controlled* by a screw.
   Active: We can adjust spring calipers more easily than stiff-jointed calipers.
   Passive: Spring calipers *can be adjusted* more easily than stiff-jointed calipers.

Because spring calipers *are controlled* by means of a screw, they *can be* more easily *adjusted* than the stiff-jointed kind.

Here is a list of the past participles of irregular verbs which you will need in the exercise.
draw – drawn, grind – ground, keep – kept, take – taken, hold – held.

1. Active: We first measure the angle.
   Passive: The angle . . . first. . . .
   Active: We then transfer the angle to the workpiece using a bevel gauge.
   Passive: The angle . . . then . . . to the workpiece using a bevel gauge.

   When scribing an angle on to a workpiece, the angle . . . first . . . and afterwards it . . . to the workpiece using a bevel gauge.

2. Active: We accurately punch small dots along the scribed line.
   Passive: Small dots . . . accurately . . . along the scribed line.
   Active: We have carried out machining.
   Passive: Machining . . . out.
   Active: We have worked to the marking out.
   Passive: The marking out . . . to.

   Small dots . . . accurately . . . along the scribed line so that, when machining . . . out, the dots show that the marking out . . . to.

3. *Marking out for drilling.*
   Active: We set the work up on the marking-out table.
   Passive: The work . . . on the marking-out table.
   Active: We draw horizontal lines through the centres using a surface
             gauge.
   Passive: Horizontal lines . . . through the centres using a surface gauge.
   Active: We then turn the work at right angles.
   Passive: The work . . . then . . . at right angles.
   Active: We draw lines through the centres again, perpendicular to those
             already drawn.
   Passive: Lines . . . through the centres again, perpendicular to those
             already drawn.

   The work . . . on the marking-out table and horizontal lines . . . through the centres using a surface gauge. The work . . . then . . . at right angles and lines . . . through the centres again, perpendicular to those already drawn.

4. Active: We use a vernier height-gauge for accurate marking out.
   Passive: A vernier height-gauge . . . for accurate marking out.
   Active: We can also use a vernier height-gauge for measuring the height of
             a surface above the marking-out table.
   Passive: A vernier height-gauge . . . also . . . for measuring the height of a
             surface above the marking-out table.

   A vernier height-gauge . . . for accurate marking out. It . . . also . . . for measuring the height of a surface above the marking-out table.

5. Active: We should grind a scriber to a sharp point before marking out.
   Passive: A scriber . . . to a sharp point before marking out.
   Active: We should scribe lines on the work as fine as possible.
   Passive: Lines . . . on the work as fine as possible.

   A scriber . . . to a sharp point before marking out because lines . . . on the work as fine as possible.

6. Active: We should wipe the surfaces of bright mild steel to remove oil and grease when marking out.
   Passive: The surfaces of bright mild steel . . . to remove oil and grease when marking out.
   Active: We should rub the surfaces with emery cloth to brighten the metal.
   Passive: The surfaces . . . with emery cloth to brighten the metal.
   Active: We should then apply a marking-out medium, such as a solution of copper sulphate.
   Passive: A marking-out medium, such as a solution of copper sulphate . . . then . . ..
   Active: We allow the solution to dry completely.
   Passive: The solution . . . to dry completely.
   Active: The film of copper enables us to see the scribed lines more clearly.
   Passive: The film of copper enables the scribed lines . . . more clearly.
   Active: We have deposited a film of copper on the surface.
   Passive: A film of copper . . . on the surface.

   When marking out on bright mild steel, the surfaces . . . to remove oil and grease and then . . . with emery cloth to brighten the metal. A marking-out medium, such as a solution of copper sulphate, . . . then . . . and . . . to dry completely. The film of copper which . . . on the surface enables the scribed lines . . . more clearly.

7. Active: We must keep the surface of a marking-out table in perfect condition.
   Passive: The surface of the marking-out table . . . in perfect condition.
   Active: We should protect the surface with a film of oil when we are not using it.
   Passive: The surface . . . with a film of oil when we are not using it.
   Active: We should take care when placing the tools on it.
   Passive: Care . . . when placing the tools on it.
   Active: We should never drop tools on it.
   Passive: Tools . . . never . . . on it.

   The surface of the marking-out table . . . in perfect condition and . . . . . . with a film of oil when it . . . .. Care . . . when placing tools on it and tools . . . never . . . on it.

8. Active: We hold the scriber at an angle to the straight edge.
   Passive: The scriber . . . at an angle to the straight edge.
   Active: We incline the scriber in the direction of movement.
   Passive: The scriber . . . in the direction of movement.

   When using a steel scriber on a straight edge, the scriber . . . at an angle
   to the straight edge and . . . in the direction of movement.

3 Bench work

---

[1]A fitter works in a fitting workshop. [2]The operations that he performs include hacksawing, chiselling and filing. [3]He works on a heavy, rigid, bench which has a vice bolted on it. [4]He has various hand tools to work with. [5]These include files and chisels. [6]The fitting workshop usually contains a marking-out table and a drilling machine. [7]The former is used for marking out before the operations mentioned above are performed. [8]The latter is used for machining holes in the work.

(a) The fitter performs only the operations of hacksawing, chiselling and filing.
(b) A fitter's hand tools consist of files and chisels.
(c) A drilling machine is used for machining holes in the work.
(d) Hacksawing, chiselling and filing are done before marking out.

[9]For certain types of work, the fitter uses grinding machines. [10]A surface grinder is used for producing a smooth surface by removing small amounts of metal. [11]This operation is called finishing work, or producing a finish. [12]In order to sharpen tools such as cold chisels and screwdrivers an off-hand grinder may be used. [13]For this kind of work, extreme accuracy is not required. [14]Both machines are operated by electricity.

(e) A surface grinder is operated by electricity.
(f) Grinding machines can be used for all types of work.

[15]A basic operation in the fitting workshop is the cutting of metal bars to the approximate length and shape required. [16]For this operation a hacksaw is used. [17]A hacksaw consists of a steel frame and a blade. [18]The blade can be made tighter or looser by turning a small wing nut at one end of the frame. [19]When this nut is tightened, the tension in the blade is increased and when it is loosened, it is decreased. [20]There are different types of hacksaw blade according to the number of teeth per inch. [21]For general use, one with 18 t.p.i. is satisfactory; for cutting thin sheet metal a fine blade of 30 t.p.i. is

better. [22]Some hacksaw blades are made from steel which has been made harder throughout. [23]Others, called flexible blades, are hardened only along the teeth.

(g)   Only flexible blades are hardened along the teeth.
(h)   A hacksaw blade can be tightened or loosened by turning a wing nut.
(i)   All hacksaw blades are made from hardened steel.

[24]Filing is one of the most important operations in bench work. [25]Different files are of different lengths; they vary also according to type and grade of cut; or they can be classified according to shape—for example, round files, square files and triangular files. [26]All files consist of a body, a tang and a handle which can be detached. [27]They are made from high carbon steel; they are very brittle, and therefore can break easily. [28]The cutting action of a file is like that of a saw. [29]It only cuts when it is moving forwards. [30]The file should be pressed down with both hands on the forward stroke. [31]On the return stroke, it should be slightly raised.

(j)   A file does not cut on the return stroke.
(k)   Files and saws cut in similar ways.
(l)   Filing is the most important operation in bench work.

Solutions

(a)   The operations that the fitter performs include hacksawing, chiselling and filing. (2)
i.e.   The fitter performs not only hacksawing, chiselling and filing, but also other operations.
i.e.   It is NOT TRUE to say that the fitter performs only the operations of hacksawing, chiselling and filing.

(b)   These (i.e. hand tools) include files and chisels. (5)
    He (i.e. the fitter) has various hand tools to work with. (4)
∴   A fitter's hand tools include files and chisels.
    include ≠ consist of (see Unit 2, Exercise F)
i.e.   A fitter's tools consist not only of files and chisels, but also of scrapers, hammers etc. (see **(a)** above)
∴   It is NOT TRUE to say that a fitter's hand tools consist of files and chisels.

(c)   The fitting workshop usually contains a marking-out table and a drilling machine. (6)
    The former is used for marking out . . . (7). The latter is used for machining holes in the work. (8)
    The former refers to a marking-out table and *the latter* refers to a drilling machine.
∴   *A drilling machine is used for machining holes in the work.*

(d) (A marking-out table) is used for marking out before the operations mentioned above are performed. (7)

The operations mentioned above refer to hacksawing, chiselling and filing. (2)

i.e. A marking-out table is used for marking out before hacksawing, chiselling and filing are performed.

i.e. first, marking out, then, hacksawing etc.

∴ Hacksawing, chiselling and filing are NOT done before marking out.

(e) Both machines are operated by electricity. (14)

i.e. Both a surface grinder (10) and an off-hand grinder (12) are operated by electricity.

∴ *A surface grinder is operated by electricity.*

(f) For certain types of work, the fitter uses grinding machines. (9)

for certain types = for some types, but not for all

i.e. Grinding machines can be used for some types of work. (e.g. finishing or sharpening tools (11, 12))

but Grinding machines CANNOT be used for all types of work.

(g) Some hacksaw blades are made from steel which has been made harder throughout. (22)

throughout i.e. all the blade has been made harder; all the blade = including the teeth

Others, called flexible blades, are hardened only along the teeth. (23)

i.e. All hacksaw blades are hardened along the teeth, but some are hardened throughout.

∴ It is NOT TRUE to say that only flexible blades are hardened along the teeth.

(h) The blade (i.e. of a hacksaw) can be made tighter or looser by turning a small wing nut at one end of the frame. (18)

can be made tighter or looser = can be tightened or loosened (19)

∴ *A hacksaw blade can be tightened or loosened by turning a wing nut.*

(i) Some hacksaw blades are made from steel which has been made harder throughout. (22)

i.e. Not all hacksaw blades are made from steel which has been hardened throughout.

e.g. Others, called flexible blades, are hardened only along the teeth. (23)

Steel which has not been made harder or steel which has been hardened = hardened steel.

∴ It is NOT TRUE to say that all hacksaw blades are made from hardened steel.

(j) It (i.e. a file) only cuts when it is moving forwards. (29)
i.e. It does not cut when it is moving backwards.
      when it is moving backwards = on the return stroke (31)
i.e. A file does NOT cut on the return stroke.

(k) The cutting action of a file is like that of a saw. (28)
=   The cutting action of files is like that of saws.
      is like = is similar to
      the cutting action = the way it cuts/the way they cut
∴.   The way files cut is similar to the way saws cut.
=   *Files and saws cut in similar ways.*

(l) Filing is one of the most important operations . . . (24)
∴.   There are other important operations. e.g. chiselling, drilling etc.
      one of the most ≠ the most
∴.   It is NOT TRUE to say that filing is the most important operation in
      bench work.

EXERCISE A *Contextual reference*

1. In sentence 11, *this operation* refers to:
    (a) producing a smooth surface
    (b) removing small amounts of metal
    (c) a surface grinder
2. In sentence 13, *this kind of work* refers to:
    (a) producing a finish
    (b) sharpening tools
    (c) finishing work
3. In sentence 21, *one* refers to:
    (a) a blade
    (b) a number of teeth per inch
    (c) a hacksaw blade
4. In sentence 25, *they* refers to:
    (a) operations
    (b) lengths
    (c) files
5. In sentence 27, *they* refers to:
    (a) files
    (b) a body, a tang and a handle
    (c) a tang and a handle
6. In sentence 28, *that* refers to:
    (a) the cutting action
    (b) a file
7. In sentence 31, *it* refers to:
    (a) the file
    (b) the return stroke

EXERCISE B *Rephrasing*

Rewrite the following, using words and constructions from the text to replace those printed in italics. For an example see Unit 1, Exercise B.

1. A fitter works on a bench which has a vice *attached to it with bolts.*
2. *A machine which is used for drilling* can usually be found in the fitting workshop.
3. A surface grinder is used for *producing a finish on* work.
4. An off-hand grinder may be used for sharpening tools as *the need to be very exact in cutting the metal* is not required.
5. *A very important* operation in bench work is hacksawing.
6. When the wing nut on the hacksaw frame is *made tighter* there is an increase in the tension in the blade.
7. Files are made from high carbon steel and *can break easily.*
8. Files *can be divided into different groups* according to length, shape, and type and grade of cut.
9. The file should be pressed down with both hands *as it is moving forward over the metal*, but *as it is moving backwards over the metal* it should be slightly raised.

EXERCISE C *Relationships between statements*

Place the following words or phrases in the sentences indicated. Replace, re-order and add to the words in the sentences where necessary. For examples, see Unit 1, Exercise C.

(a) such as (4+5)   (f) but (21)
(b) for example (10)   (g) however (23)
(c) however (12)   (h) we may compare . . . to . . . (28)
(d) because (12+13)   (i) therefore (30)
(c) may be classified (20)   (j) on the other hand (31)

EXERCISE D *Definitions of operations*

Part 1 A number of common hand tools have names which are also used in the *-ing* form to describe the operation they perform.

EXAMPLE

Name of tool	Name of operation
file	filing

(i) A file is a tool *which is used for removing metal* in order to produce a smooth surface.
(ii) Filing is an operation *by which metal is removed* in order to produce a smooth surface.

(i) is a definition of a tool – a file.
(ii) is a definition of an operation – filing

Below are definitions of common hand tools. Write definitions of the operations which these hand tools perform.

EXAMPLE
  A scraper is a tool *which is used for removing* slight irregularities on a flat surface.
∴ Scraping is an operation *by which* slight irregularities on a flat surface *are removed*.

(a) A chisel is a tool which is used for chipping away excess material from a large surface.
(b) A hacksaw is a tool which is used for cutting metal bars and strips.
(c) A hand-drill is a machine which is used for machining a hole in a work-piece.
(d) An off-hand grinder is a machine which is used for sharpening hand tools.
(e) A reamer is a tool which is used for enlarging and finishing a hole to size.
(f) A scriber is a tool which is used for marking out cutting dimensions.
(g) A rivet is a metal pin which is used for joining metal to metal mechanically.

Part 2

Instead of saying *an operation by which* we can say:
     (i) an operation whereby,
OR (ii) a process by which,
OR (iii) a process whereby.
Express the definitions you have made in Part 1 above, in this way.

Part 3

Complete this table:

	INSTRUMENT, TOOL *or* MACHINE	VERB	PROCESS *or* OPERATION
(a)	file	to file	filing
(b)	chisel	. . .	. . .
(c)	. . .	. . .	scraping
(d)	. . .	to drill	. . .
(e)	hacksaw	. . .	. . .
(f)	reamer	. . .	. . .
(g)	. . .	. . .	grinding
(h)	. . .	to scribe	. . .
(i)	rivet	. . .	. . .
(j)	. . .	to tap	. . .
(k)	. . .	. . .	screwing
(l)	bender	. . .	. . .
(m)	lathe	to turn	. . .
(n)	soldering iron	to solder	. . .
(o)	cold chisel	to chip	. . .

EXERCISE E *Generalizations*

Part 1 Look at this diagram:

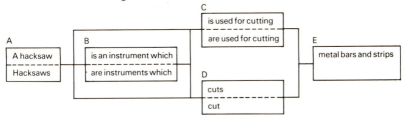

From this diagram we can make (i) definitions or (ii) generalizations, as follows:

(i) DEFINITIONS: A+B+C+E

A hacksaw is an instrument which is used for cutting metal bars and strips.

Hacksaws are instruments which are used for cutting metal bars and strips.

(ii) GENERALIZATIONS: A+C+E

A hacksaw is used for cutting metal bars and strips.

Hacksaws are used for cutting metal bars and strips.

    OR A+D+E

A hacksaw cuts metal bars and strips.

Hacksaws cut metal bars and strips.

1. Draw the two diagrams below and complete them, then write definitions and generalizations from them.

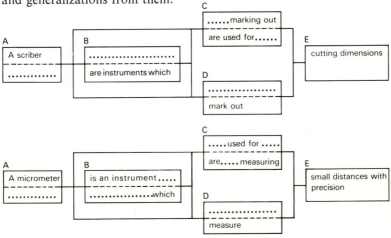

2. Draw diagrams and write definitions and generalizations for the following: (a) a scraper, (b) a chisel, (c) a reamer, (d) a rivet.

Part 2 There are other ways in which we can make statements which are generalizations about the use of certain tools.

EXAMPLES

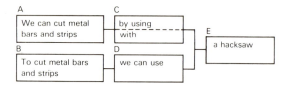

A+C+E = We can cut metal bars and strips by using a hacksaw.
         We can cut metal bars and strips with a hacksaw.
B+D+E = To cut metal bars and strips we can use a hacksaw.
D+E+B = We can use a hacksaw to cut metal bars and strips.

Make generalizations using the information in the following diagrams, as shown in the examples above.

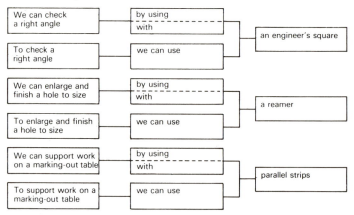

Part 3 We can make generalizations about operations in the fitting workshop as follows:

EXAMPLES

DEFINITION

Hacksawing is an operation by which (*or* whereby) metal bars and strips are cut.

GENERALIZATIONS

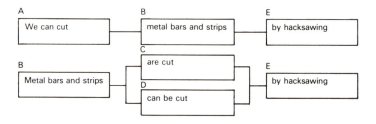

A+B+E = We can cut metal bars and strips by hacksawing.
B+C+E = Metal bars and strips are cut by hacksawing.
B+D+E = Metal bars and strips can be cut by hacksawing.

Write generalizations about the following operations. Use the information in Exercise D, Part 1.
(a) chiselling, (b) scraping, (c) filing, (d) riveting, (e) reaming, (f) drilling.

EXERCISE F *Writing descriptions from information in a table*
Study the following table, which gives information about different types of file.

	Name	Use	Cross-sectional shape	Sides	Type and grade of cut	
1.	Hand file	general surfacing work		parallel	both faces one edge other edge	
2.	Square file	filing square corners		tapered	all faces	
3.	Round file	opening out holes and rounding corners		tapered	smooth grades rough grades	
4.	Flat file	general surfacing work		tapered	both faces both sides	
5.	Half round	filing concave surfaces		tapered	flat face curved face	
6.	Rasp file	filing soft metal		parallel	both faces	
7.	Triangular file	filing corners of 60° to 90°		tapered	all faces	
8.	Knife file	filing corners of less than 60°		tapered	side faces narrow edge	

Types of cut: single cut, double cut, rasp cut, uncut

Now write short descriptions of each type of file illustrated below. Use the information given in the table above, and construct your description as in the example.

EXAMPLE
A hand file is used for general surfacing work. It is rectangular in cross-sectional shape, with parallel sides. Both faces are double cut, one edge is uncut and the other edge is single cut.

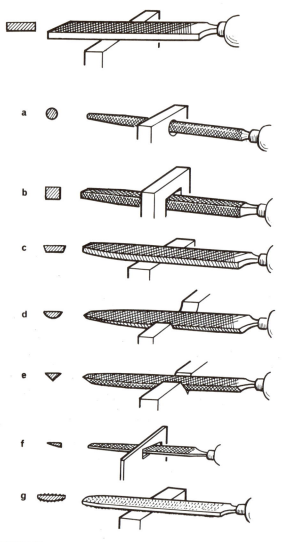

II GRAMMAR

EXERCISE A *The use of* to+infinitive *in the expression of purpose*

We can express the purpose for which something is done by using *to + infinitive*. When we state our *purpose* in doing something, we are stating our *reason* for doing it, or our *object* or *aim* in doing it.

EXAMPLES

(i) We use a hacksaw in the fitting workshop. *Our purpose in using it* is to cut metal bars and strips.

= (a) *We use* a hacksaw in the fitting workshop *to cut* metal bars and strips.
= (b) A hacksaw *is used* in the fitting workshop *to cut* metal bar sand strips.

(ii) We keep micrometers in boxes. *Our object in doing this* is to protect them from rust and dust.
= (a) *We keep* micrometers in boxes *to protect* them from rust and dust.
= (b) Micrometers *are kept* in boxes *to protect* them from rust and dust.

Rewrite the following sentences as in the examples above.
1. We set the teeth of a hacksaw at angles. Our purpose in doing this is to make a cut which is wider than the blade.
   (a) We set the teeth of the hacksaw at angles . . . a cut which is wider than the blade.
   (b) The teeth of the hacksaw . . . at angles . . . a cut which is wider than the blade.
2. We place the workpiece in the vice as low as possible. Our reason for doing this is to avoid vibration and screeching.
   (a) We place the workpiece in the vice as low as possible . . . vibration and screeching.
   (b) The workpiece . . . as low as possible in the vice . . . vibration and screeching.
3. We tighten the wing nut at one end of the frame. The object of doing this is to increase the tension in the blade. (Note: The object of doing = Our object in doing)
   (a) We tighten the wing nut at one end of the frame . . . the tension in the blade.
   (b) The wing nut at one end of the frame . . . . . . the tension in the blade.
4. We anneal steel. Our aim in doing this to make it as soft as possible.
   (a) We anneal steel . . . it as soft as possible.
   (b) Steel . . . . . . it as soft as possible.
5. We use the method of draw-filing. Our purpose in using it is to produce a good finish on a narrow surface.
   (a) We can use the method of draw-filing . . . a good finish on a narrow surface.
   (b) The method of draw-filing . . . . . . a good finish on a narrow surface.

EXERCISE B *The use of* in order to+infinitive *and* so as to+infinitive *in the expression of purpose*
Instead of *to+infinitive* we may use *in order to+infinitive* or *so as to+infinitive* to express purpose.

EXAMPLE
   We should adopt the correct stance at the vice. *The reason for doing this* is to maintain our balance while filing. (Note: The reason for doing this = Our reason for doing this.)

= The correct stance *should be adopted* at the vice *in order to* maintain our balance while filing.

OR The correct stance should be adopted at the vice *so as to* maintain our balance while filing.

Join the following pairs of sentences together, using the passive form of the verb followed by (a) *in order to* and (b) *so as to*, as in the example above.

1. We should wear gloves when filing. The reason for wearing them is to protect our hands.
2. You should raise the file on its return stroke. Doing this enables you to prevent the dulling of the cutting teeth.
3. You should rub chalk into the teeth of the file during finishing work. The purpose of doing so is to prevent bits of metal clogging the teeth. (Note: The purpose of doing = Our purpose in doing)
4. You should insert the hacksaw blade with the teeth pointing away from the handle. The object of doing this is to cut material on the forward stroke.
5. Manufacturers machine the top of a marking-out table flat. The object of doing this is to provide a good working surface.

EXERCISE C *The statement of purpose in the first part of a sentence*

Very often the purpose needs to be stated first. The reason for doing this is to emphasize its importance as the purpose of, or reason for, doing something.

EXAMPLE

We want to check an internal right angle. *So*, we hold the stock firmly on the datum surface.

= (a) *To check* an internal right angle, *we hold* the stock firmly on the datum surface

= (b) *To check* an internal right angle, the stock *is held* firmly on the datum surface.

= (c) *In order to* check an internal right angle, the stock *is held* firmly on the datum surface.

Join the following pairs of sentences together in the three ways shown in the example given above.

1. We want to check the flatness of a surface, and its squareness to the face of the work. So we should first use a try-square and rule.
2. We need to produce an internal thread by means of a tap. So we must first drill a hole of a diameter which is equal to the diameter at the bottom of the tap thread.

3. We have to avoid damage to any finished surfaces on a workpiece by the hardened jaw pieces of the vice. So we use false jaws of a softer metal, or even wood.
4. It is necessary to avoid crooked hacksawing. Therefore, make sure you have tightened the blade sufficiently.
5. We should be careful to avoid breaking files and blunting their teeth. Therefore, we should put them carefully in a tool box or on a rack.
6. We want to show up a line very clearly. Therefore, we brush the surfaces of the component with a suitable marking-out medium.
7. A particular file has to be identified. Therefore, we should know the shape, and type and grade of cut of the files we use.
8. We are required to mark out accurately. So we must draw the lines with a scriber as fine as possible.
9. Tubes or thin sheet metal are to be cut. Therefore, we should use a hacksaw blade with 30 t.p.i.
10. We want to mark the location of holes to be drilled. So we use a centre punch in conjunction with a hammer.

EXERCISE D *The use of* so that+clause *in the expression of result and purpose*

Another way of stating the purpose of doing something is to state the *result* or *consequence* of doing it. We can do this by using the expression *so that* to join statements together.

EXAMPLES
   (i) We keep micrometers in boxes. *This enables us* to protect them from rust and dust.
= (a) *We keep* micrometers in boxes *so that we can protect them* from rust and dust.
= (b) Micrometers *are kept* in boxes *so that they can be protected* from rust and dust.
   (ii) We place a workpiece in the vice as low as possible. *The result of doing this* is that we avoid vibration and screeching.
= (a) *We place* a workpiece in the vice as low as possible *so that we avoid* vibration and screeching.
= (b) A workpiece *is placed* as low as possible in the vice *so that* vibration and screeching *are avoided.*

Join the following statements together using *so that* as in (i) and (ii) above, using the active and passive forms of the verb. Note that the expressions printed in italics are omitted.

1. We set the teeth of a hacksaw at angles. *This enables us* to make a cut which is wider than the blade.

2. We tighten the wing nut at one end of the frame. *The result of doing this* is that we increase the tension in the blade.
3. We use the method of draw-filing. *This enables us* to produce a good finish on a narrow surface.
4. We hold the handle of a hammer at the end and not close to the head. *Doing this* will enable us to exercise greater control.
5. We anneal steel. *The result of annealing it* is that we make it as soft as possible.
6. We should adopt the correct stance at the vice. *This enables* the filing arm to move freely.
7. A common fault when filing a flat surface is that we do not hold the file horizontally. *The result is* that we produce a convex surface.
8. You should raise the file on its return stroke. *If you do this*, you prevent the dulling of the cutting teeth.
9. We must keep file teeth as sharp as possible. *The result of doing this* is that they cut metal effectively.

4 Metals and their properties

I READING AND COMPREHENSION

---

[1]We may distinguish two groups of metals. [2]Those which contain mainly iron are called ferrous metals, and those in which the basic material is a metal other than iron are termed non-ferrous metals. [3]The former include cast iron, wrought iron, and steel. [4]Copper, tin, zinc and lead are examples of non-ferrous metals. [5]When some metals are combined, they form an alloy. [6]Non-ferrous alloys include brass, which is made from copper and zinc, and bronze, which is made from copper and tin.

(a) The basic material of ferrous metals is iron.
(b) Metals can be combined to form an alloy.
(c) Examples of non-ferrous alloys are brass and bronze.

[7]Cast iron is really an alloy of iron and carbon. [8]It is made from pig iron which has been remelted and made purer. [9]Cast iron is, then, refined pig iron. [10]The amount of carbon in cast iron is reduced to between $2\frac{1}{2}$ and 4 per cent. [11]As cast iron is very brittle, it will not bend. [12]It cannot be forged, either. [13]On the other hand, it is easily shaped by casting and some types can be easily machined. [14]Cast iron is used for making surface plates, vee blocks and marking-out tables.

(d) Cast iron can be neither forged nor bent.
(e) The carbon content of cast iron is $2\frac{1}{2}$–4%.
(f) Cast iron is made from pig iron which has been refined.

[15]Steel is basically an iron-carbon alloy, too. [16]It is made by reducing the carbon content of pig iron to amounts which are exactly known. [17]It can also be made by adding known amounts of carbon to almost pure iron. [18]If only carbon is added, plain carbon steels are produced. [19]If other elements are added, alloy steels are produced. [20]Stainless steel contains both nickel and chromium, and the main element added to make most types of high speed steel is tungsten.

(g) There is nickel and chromium in stainless steel.

(h) Alloy steels contain elements in addition to iron and carbon.

[21]Plain carbon steels may be classified according to their carbon content. [22]Low carbon, or mild, steel has up to 0·25% carbon in it. [23]It is easily cut, filed and drilled, and it can be forged. [24]Medium carbon steel contains between 0·25 and 0·5% carbon. [25]Darker and stronger than mild steel, it is used for things which have to be tough. [26]High carbon steel has a carbon content of 0·5 to 1·3%. [27]It is a dark steel and it is very strong. [28]It is used for making files, centre punches and hacksaw blades. [29]It is known as tool steel.

(i) Mild steel has up to 0·25% carbon in it.

(j) Tool steel has up to 1·3% carbon in it.

(k) Medium carbon steel has a carbon content of between 0·25 and 0·5%.

(l) Mild steel contains more than 0·25% carbon.

Solutions

(a) Those (i.e. groups of metals) which contain mainly iron are called ferrous metals. (2)

i.e. Ferrous metals contain mainly iron.
which contain mainly iron = of which the basic material is iron
. . . those (i.e. groups of metals) in which the basic material is a metal other than iron are termed non-ferrous metals. (2)
a metal other than iron = a metal which is not iron

∴ *The basic material of ferrous metals is iron.*

(b) When some metals are combined, they form an alloy. (5)

= Some metals can be combined to form an alloy. (see Unit 3, Grammar)
SOME metals i.e. not ALL metals

but Metals can be combined to form an alloy = ALL metals can be combined to form an alloy.

∴ It is NOT TRUE to say that metals (i.e. all metals) can be combined to form an alloy.

(c) Non-ferrous alloys include brass . . . and bronze. (6)

i.e. Brass and bronze are examples of non-ferrous alloys.

= *Examples of non-ferrous alloys are brass and bronze.*

(d) (Cast iron) will not bend (11). It cannot be forged, either. (12)

= Cast iron cannot be bent and it cannot be forged.

= Cast iron can neither be bent nor forged.

= *Cast iron can neither be forged nor bent.*

(e) The amount of carbon in cast iron is reduced to between $2\frac{1}{2}$ and 4 per cent. (10)

∴ The amount of carbon in cast iron is between $2\frac{1}{2}$ and 4 per cent.
between $2\frac{1}{2}$ and 4 per cent $= 2\frac{1}{2}$–4%
the amount of carbon in cast iron = the carbon content of cast iron

∴ *The carbon content of cast iron is $2\frac{1}{2}$–4%.*

(f) It (i.e. cast iron) is made from pig iron which has been remelted and made purer. (8)
Cast iron is, then (=therefore), refined pig iron. (9)

∴ remelted and made purer = refined
refined pig iron = pig iron which has been refined

∴ *Cast iron is made from pig iron which has been refined.*

(g) [X Stainless steel] [Y contains] both [Z nickel and chromium]. (20)
= [Y There is] [Z nickel and chromium] [X in stainless steel].
There is nickel and chromium in stainless steel.

(h) If only carbon is added (to pig iron (16)) plain carbon steels are produced. (18)
If other elements are added, alloy steels are produced. (19)
= Alloy steels are produced if other elements are added.

i.e. Alloy steels are produced if other elements are added to iron and carbon.
other elements are added to iron and carbon = there are elements in addition to iron and carbon

∴ *Alloy steels contain elements in addition to iron and carbon.*

(i) Low carbon, or mild, steel has up to 0·25% carbon in it. (22)
i.e. Low carbon steel is also called mild steel. (see Unit 1, solution (a))
∴ *Mild steel has up to 0·25% carbon in it.*

(j) High carbon steel has a carbon content of 0·5% to 1·3%. (26)
High carbon steel is known as tool steel. (29)
∴ Tool steel has a carbon content of 0·5% to 1·3%.
of 0·5% to 1·3% = of up to 1·3%
∴ *Tool steel has up to 1·3% carbon in it.*

(k) Medium carbon steel contains between 0·25 and 0·5% carbon. (24)
contains . . . carbon = has a carbon content (see 26)
∴ *Medium carbon steel has a carbon content of between 0·25 and 0·5%.*

(l) Low carbon, or mild, steel has up to 0·25% carbon in it. (22)
has up to = has no more than
i.e. Mild steel has no more than 0·25% carbon in it.
has . . . in it = contains
i.e. Mild steel DOES NOT contain more than 0·25% carbon.

EXERCISE A *Contextual reference*

1. In sentence 2, *those* refers to:
   (a) groups of metals
   (b) ferrous metals
2. In sentence 3, *the former* refers to:
   (a) non-ferrous metals
   (b) ferrous metals
   (c) groups of metals
3. In sentence 5, *they* refers to:
   (a) some metals
   (b) non-ferrous metals
   (c) copper, tin and zinc
4. In sentence 23, *it* refers to:
   (a) plain carbon steel
   (b) low carbon steel
   (c) mild steel
5. In sentence 25, *it* refers to:
   (a) medium carbon steel
   (b) mild steel
6. In sentence 29 *it* refers to:
   (a) mild steel
   (b) high carbon steel
   (c) medium carbon steel.

EXERCISE B *Rephrasing*

Rewrite the following, using words and constructions from the text to replace those printed in italics.

1. The *main element* of ferrous metals is iron.
2. Non-ferrous *metals which are combined* include brass and bronze.
3. Cast iron is made from pig iron which has been *remelted and made purer*.
4. Cast iron *breaks easily*.
5. Cast iron can be easily given a shape by *pouring the molten metal into a mould*.
6. Steel can be made by adding *certain amounts of carbon which are exactly known* to almost pure iron.
7. Plain carbon steels may be *divided up into groups on the basis of* their carbon content.

EXERCISE C *Relationships between statements*

Place the following expressions in the sentences indicated. Replace and re-order the words in the sentence where necessary.

(a) namely . . . namely (1+2)
(b) whereas (3+4)
(c) for example (6)
(d) in other words (9)

(e) so (11)
(f) nor (11+12)
(g) however (13)
(h) therefore (14)
(i) alternatively (17)

(j) however (19)
(k) for example (20)
(l) consequently (28)
(m) and for this reason (28+29)

EXERCISE D *Classification and levels of generalization*

Part 1

Draw the following diagram and fill in the blank spaces, using information contained in the texts.

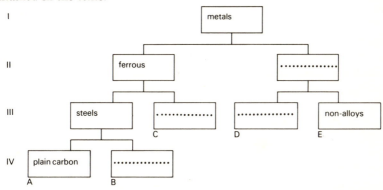

The diagram is a *classification* of metals. There are 4 levels of *generalization*.
Items at a higher level are more general than items at a lower level.
Items at a lower level belong to *classes* of items which are at a higher level.
We may add a fifth level which represents *examples* of the classes of metals at the third and fourth levels.

Part 2

Arrange the following examples of metals in their correct classes, labelled A, B, C, D, E in the diagram above. For example, (a) *mild steel* is A (i.e. a kind of plain carbon steel).

(a) mild steel
(b) copper
(c) high speed steel
(d) cast iron
(e) aluminium

(f) wrought iron
(g) zinc
(h) bronze
(i) stainless steel
(j) lead

(k) medium carbon steel
(l) tool steel
(m) brass
(n) tin
(o) silver steel

Part 3

Write as many simple definitions as possible of the metals in the list in Part 2, above.
First, study the following examples carefully.

EXAMPLES
Mild steel *is a* plain carbon steel.
Mild steel *is a* ferrous metal.
Mild steel *belongs to a class of metals called* plain carbon steels.
Mild steel *may be classed* as a plain carbon steel.

Part 4

Classify the following items in the form of diagrams as in Part 1 above.
(a) workshop materials – metallic – non-metallic – ferrous – non-ferrous – wood – plastics – iron – steel – tin – copper.
(b) hand tools – cutting – hitting – single cutting edge – multiple cutting edges – hammers – mallets – chisels – scrapers – files – hacksaws.
(c) metal joining methods – soldering – welding – riveting – soft soldering – silver soldering – brazing – oxy-acetylene – electric arc.
(d) engineer's instruments – measuring – marking out – steel rule – micrometer – vernier calipers – scriber – dividers.
(e) plain carbon steels – low carbon steels – black mild steel – bright drawn mild steel – medium carbon steels – high carbon steels – tool steel – silver steel.
(f) pig iron – wrought iron – cast iron – grey iron – white iron – malleable cast iron.
(g) weight unit – metric unit – non-metric unit – kilogram – gram – pound – ounce – ton – stone.
(h) measuring unit – metric unit – non-metric unit – kilometre – metre – centimetre – millimetre – yard – mile – foot – inch.
(i) timber – hardwoods – softwoods – oak – beech – mahogany – white wood – red wood – spruce – pitch pine.

Part 5

Study the following tables carefully.

(a)

Metals	can be	divided into two	classes: groups: kinds:	ferrous and non-ferrous.
	may be	divided into classified as		

(b)

Two	groups classes types kinds	of metal	can be may be	distinguished: ferrous and non-ferrous.

(c) Ferrous metals	include	steel, cast iron,
	include metals such as	wrought iron etc.
	are of two types,	steels and irons.

1. Write down and complete the following paragraph using the information from the diagram in Parts 1 and 2 above.
   Note that many of the sentences are similar in construction to those in the tables given above.
   Metals can be classified as . . . and . . .. The former may be divided into steels and . . ., while non-ferrous metals may be divided into . . . such as . . . and . . ., and non-alloys, or pure metals, such as . . ., . . . and . . . . Two kinds of steel may be distinguished: . . . steels and . . . steels. Examples of the former include . . . steel and . . . steel. . . . steel and . . . steel are examples of alloy steels.
2. Using the patterns given in the tables above, write out classifications of the items which you have arranged in diagrams in Part 4.

EXAMPLES
   (i) Workshop materials can be divided into two main classes: metallic and non-metallic. There are two types of metallic material, ferrous and non-ferrous. Non-metallic materials include wood and plastics. Examples of ferrous metals are iron and steel. Non-ferrous materials include metals such as tin and copper.
OR (ii) Workshop materials may be classified as metallic and non-metallic. Two kinds of metallic material can be distinguished: ferrous metals, such as iron and steel, and non-ferrous – such as tin and copper. Non-metallic materials include wood and plastics.

Part 6

A statement which uses a higher level item is more general than a statement which uses lower level items. In the following statements (i) is more general than (ii), (ii) is more general than (iii), and (iii) is more general than (iv).

 (i) *Tools* are made from steel.
 (ii) *Hand tools* are made from steel.
(iii) *A file* is made from steel.
(iv) *A round file* is made from steel.

Note that if (i) is true, then (ii), (iii) and (iv) are also true.

1. Change the following statements into higher level generalizations. In brackets are the exercises in Part 4 above and the levels of generalization by reference to which you should rewrite the statement. In order to do this, refer to the classifications which you made in Part 4. Make any other changes in the sentences which are necessary.

EXAMPLE
>   *A flat file* is made from high carbon steel. [b, level 3]
> ∴   Hand tools with multiple cutting edges are made from high carbon steel.

(a) Hand tools are usually made from *hardened tool steel*. [e, level 2]
(b) *Diamond-point chisels* are used for removing metal and should be kept sharp. [b, level 2]
(c) The basic materials in *malleable cast iron* are iron and carbon. [f, level 1]
(d) *Copper* expands when it is heated. [a, level 2]
(e) *A scriber* should be kept free from rust and dust. [d, level 1]
(f) *Odd-leg calipers* are made from tool steel. [d, level 2]
(g) *Oxy-acetylene welding* can be dangerous, and requires a great deal of skill and practice. [c, level 1]

2. Use the statements in 1 above and the generalizations you have made from them to make statements of the following kind.

EXAMPLE
Tools are made from tool steel.
A flat file is a tool.
Therefore (∴) a flat file is made from tool steel.

EXERCISE E *Classification according to defining characteristics*

Classifications are made according to some principle of classification, and statements are made in the active or passive form.

EXAMPLES
>   (i) (a) We may classify files according to their shape.
>   (b) Files may be classified according to their shape.
>   (ii) (a) We may classify hacksaw blades according to the number of teeth per inch.
>   (b) Hacksaw blades may be classified according to the number of teeth per inch.

Such statements may be followed by examples of particular objects and a statement of their defining characteristics.

EXAMPLE

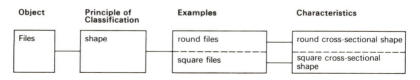

Object	Principle of Classification	Examples	Characteristics
Files	shape	round files	round cross-sectional shape
		square files	square cross-sectional shape

Files may be classified according to their shape. For example, round files have a round cross-sectional shape but square files have a square cross-sectional shape.

Part 1

Make statements about how the following objects may be classified as in the example:

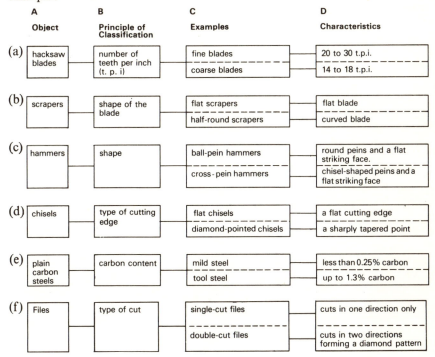

	A Object	B Principle of Classification	C Examples	D Characteristics
(a)	hacksaw blades	number of teeth per inch (t. p. i)	fine blades	20 to 30 t.p.i.
			coarse blades	14 to 18 t.p.i.
(b)	scrapers	shape of the blade	flat scrapers	flat blade
			half-round scrapers	curved blade
(c)	hammers	shape	ball-pein hammers	round peins and a flat striking face.
			cross-pein hammers	chisel-shaped peins and a flat striking face
(d)	chisels	type of cutting edge	flat chisels	a flat cutting edge
			diamond-pointed chisels	a sharply tapered point
(e)	plain carbon steels	carbon content	mild steel	less than 0.25% carbon
			tool steel	up to 1.3% carbon
(f)	Files	type of cut	single-cut files	cuts in one direction only
			double-cut files	cuts in two directions forming a diamond pattern

Part 2

Note that the order C+A+D in the exercises above produce a definition of the particular example. It is defined according to its appearance.

EXAMPLE

[C A round file] is [A a file] which has a [D round cross-sectional shape.]

Define the following, using the information given in Part 1 above.

(a) a square file
(b) a flat scraper
(c) a half-round scraper
(d) a ball-pein hammer
(e) a flat chisel

(f) a diamond-point chisel
(g) mild steel
(h) tool steel
(i) a double-cut file
(j) a single-cut file.

Part 3

There is another way of stating a principle of classification followed by examples. Study the following pattern:

[**A** Metals] may be classified according to whether they [**B** contain iron or not].

For example,

C1 in ferrous metals   D1 iron is the main constituent
C2 in non-ferrous metals   D2 there is little or no iron

The pattern can be stated as follows:

A may be classified according to whether they **B**.
For example, $C^1 + D^1$, whereas $C^2 + D^2$.

We can now read the pattern as follows:

Metals may be classified according to whether they contain iron or not. For example, in ferrous metals iron is the main constituent, whereas in non-ferrous metals there is little or no iron.

Now write out similar statements from the material in (a) and (b) below.

(a)
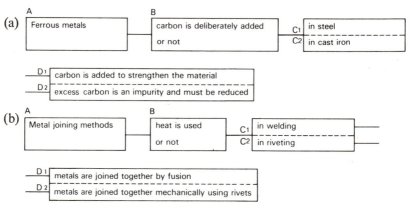
A Ferrous metals
B carbon is deliberately added / or not
C1 in steel
C2 in cast iron
D1 carbon is added to strengthen the material
D2 excess carbon is an impurity and must be reduced

(b)
A Metal joining methods
B heat is used / or not
C1 in welding
C2 in riveting
D1 metals are joined together by fusion
D2 metals are joined together mechanically using rivets

The pattern in (c)–(f) below is more complicated. First, look carefully at the material in (c).

(c)
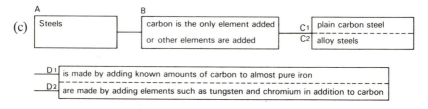
A Steels
B carbon is the only element added / or other elements are added
C1 plain carbon steel
C2 alloy steels
D1 is made by adding known amounts of carbon to almost pure iron
D2 are made by adding elements such as tungsten and chromium in addition to carbon

The pattern can be stated as follows:

A may be classified according to whether B^1 or whether B^2.

For example, C^1+D^1, whereas C^2+D^2.

We can now read (c) as follows:

Steels may be classified according to whether carbon is the only element added or whether other elements are added. For example, plain carbon steel is made by adding known amounts of carbon to almost pure iron, whereas alloy steels are made by adding elements such as tungsten and chromium in addition to carbon.

Now write out similar statements from the material in (d), (e) and (f).

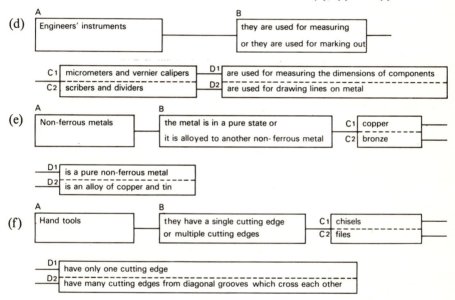

II GRAMMAR

EXERCISE A *Defining and non-defining relative clauses*

Look at this table:

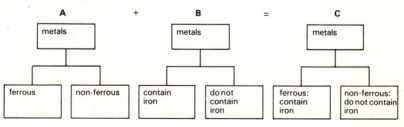

A Some metals are called ferrous metals.

B Some metals contain iron.

A+B = C Metals which contain iron are called ferrous metals.

= Ferrous metals are metals which contain iron.

A Some metals are called non-ferrous metals.

B Some metals do not contain iron.

A+B = C Metals which do not contain iron are called non-ferrous metals.

= Non-ferrous metals are metals which do not contain iron.

Expressions in which the main word is a *noun* are called *noun phrases*. If two sentences each contain a noun phrase, and the noun phrases each refer to the same thing, then the sentences can be joined together by a relative pronoun, as in the statements **C** above. In those statements the relative pronoun is *which*.

Now, compare the following sentences:
(i) A machine which is dangerous should be provided with a protective casing.
(ii) A drilling machine, which is dangerous, should be used with the drill guard down.

The first sentence is an example of a *defining relative clause*. The clause tells us what machine we are talking about: i.e. a machine which is dangerous. The second sentence is an example of a *non-defining relative clause*. In this case we know what machine we are talking about: i.e. a drilling machine. The relative clause simply tells us something *more* about the machine: i.e. . . ., a drilling machine is dangerous, ... Non-defining relative clauses are usually separated from the rest of the sentence by commas, or by brackets or by dashes.

Combine each pair of sentences into a single sentence. Change the second sentence into a relative clause and insert it into the first sentence at the point indicated by the dots. In each case say whether the relative clause is defining or non-defining.

1. A metal . . . is malleable. A metal can be spread out by hammering without cracking.
2. Bending and pressing and hammering of a metal often leads to a condition. . . . The condition is known as work hardening.
3. Brass . . . is a non-ferrous alloy. Brass is made from copper and zinc.
4. A fitter works on a heavy, rigid bench . . . . The bench has a vice bolted on it.
5. A surface grinder may be used for producing a finish on metal . . . . Metal has been cut on another machine.
6. The working head of a soldering iron is usually made of copper . . . . Copper is a good conductor of heat.

7. Some hacksaw blades are made from steel . . . Steel has been hardened throughout.

8. A micrometer is an instrument . . . . The instrument is used for measuring small distances very precisely.

9. Oxygen and acetylene, when mixed together, can produce a flame . . . . The flame reaches a temperature of about 3300° C.

10. Low carbon steel . . . contains up to 0·25% carbon. Low carbon steel is also known as mild steel.

11. The teeth of a hacksaw are set at angles so that the saw makes a cut . . . . The cut is wider than the blade.

12. There are two types of soldering iron: plain irons . . . and electric irons . . . . Plain irons have to be heated on a gas ring. Electric irons have an internal element for heating.

13. A plain steel . . . can be recognized by a stream of long white sparks . . . . A plain steel has a low carbon content. The sparks are produced when it is ground on an emery wheel.

14. Lead is a light grey metal . . . . The metal darkens quite rapidly when it is exposed to the atmosphere . . . . The atmosphere gives it a more familiar dark colour.

15. The properties of irons and steels depend on the amount of carbon . . . . Carbon has been added to them.

16. The cables . . . are called conductors. They carry electric current to the various machines and tools in a factory.

17. A hacksaw consists of a frame . . . and a blade . . . . The former may be adjustable. The latter is tensioned by a wing nut at one end of the frame.

18. The legs of spring calipers are opened or closed by means of a screw . . . . This screw is controlled by an adjusting nut.

EXERCISE B *Short-form relative clauses*

Part 1

Relative clauses often appear in a shortened form.

(i) In clauses which begin *which has* or *which have*, *with* may be used instead.

EXAMPLE

Steels which have a carbon content of between 0·5 and 1·3% are known as high carbon steels.

= Steels *with* a carbon content of between 0·5 and 1·3% are known as high carbon steels.

(ii) In clauses in which the verb is active, the *-ing* form of the verb may be used instead.

EXAMPLES

Steels *which have* a carbon content of between 0·5 and 1·3% are known as high carbon steels.

= Steels *having* a carbon content of between . . . .
Steels *which contain* between 0·5 and 1·3% of carbon are known as high carbon steels.

= Steels *containing* between 0·5 and 1·3% . . . .

(iii) In clauses in which the verb is passive, the relative pronoun and the verb *to be* can be omitted.

EXAMPLES

High carbon steel, *which is known* as tool steel, usually has more than 1% carbon in it.

= High carbon steel, *known as* tool steel . . . .
Steel *which is used* for making files, centre punches and hacksaw blades has to be very strong.

= Steel *used for* making files, centre punches . . . .

Combine each of the following pairs of sentences into a single sentence. Change the second sentence into a short-form relative clause, using one of the ways shown above, and insert it into the first sentence at the point indicated by the dots. In each case state whether the resulting construction is defining or non-defining, as in the example.

EXAMPLE

The heat . . . is produced by an electric arc.
The heat is required for welding.

= The heat *which is required for welding* is produced by an electric arc. (defining)

= The heat *required for welding* is produced by an electric arc.

1. The vice . . . must be at the correct height.
The vice holds the work on the fitter's bench.
2. Typical objects . . . include springs, hammers, shafts and axles.
Objects are made from medium carbon steel.
3. Steel is essentially an iron-carbon alloy . . . .
The alloy contains less than 1·7% carbon.
4. Wrought iron is made by remelting and refining pig iron in a small furnace. . . .
The furnace is known as a puddling furnace.
5. Nickel steels are of two types: low nickel steels . . . and high nickel steels. . . .
The former have 3–5% nickel.
The latter have 25–40% nickel.
6. The main part of a micrometer is a semi-circular frame. . . .
The frame has a barrel. . . .
The barrel is attached to one end through which a spindle screws.
7. Usually in welding, the two materials . . . are of the same composition.
They are to be joined together.

8. A flexible steel tape, . . ., rolls into a case.
   It has each inch or centimetre marked in uniform divisions.
9 A hammer consists of a head, . . ., and a shaft, ...
   One is made of cast steel . . . .
   It has a hardened striking face.
   The other is made from well-seasoned wood.
10. Bench stakes are used to support work and have many different shapes and sizes . . . .
   These shapes and sizes depend on the article . . . and the process . . . .
   An article is being made.
   A process is being carried out.

Part 2

Look at the sentences containing relative clauses which you wrote in Grammar Exercise A. Shorten the following sentences from that exercise in one of the ways shown above.

2, 3, 4, 5, 8, 9, 10, 13, 15, 16, 18.

5 The forge

---

[1]Forging is a process which takes place in a smithy. [2]It consists of heating metal and pressing or hammering it into shape. [3]Both ferrous and non-ferrous metals may be forged, but it is usually the former that are forged by hand processes. [4]The most suitable metal for this purpose is wrought iron.

(a) Forging is a process in which metal is heated and pressed or hammered into shape.
(b) All ferrous and non-ferrous metals may be forged.
(c) Only ferrous metals are forged by hand processes.
(d) Wrought iron is the best ferrous metal for hand-forging.

[5]Modern forges, or forging hearths, are made of plates of cast iron or steel. [6]Those which are made of cast iron are bolted together, whereas those which are made of steel are riveted or welded together. [7]The fire-place, which is in the middle of the hearth, is lined with fire-bricks. [8]Above the fire-place is a flue, which is in the shape of a hood and fitted with a chimney. [9]Its purpose is to carry away the fumes from the fire. [10]Behind the hearth is a blower which is driven by electric power. [11]The blower is connected to the tuyere through which a draught of air is blown into the fire. [12]The tuyere has to be cooled to prevent it from getting hot. [13]It passes through a tank of water which is known as the bosh. [14]This water tank is fitted to the back of the forge. [15]The temperature of the fire can be adjusted by varying the amount of air which enters the tuyere.

(e) A modern forging hearth is made of either cast iron or steel plates.
(f) There is a flue above the fire-place to carry away the fumes.
(g) A power-driven blower blows a draught of air through the tuyere into the fire.

[16]The anvil is the blacksmith's basic piece of equipment. [17]It is made of mild steel, and has a cast iron stand. [18]The anvil supports the work which is

to be shaped on a surface which is made of hardened steel. [19]This surface is known as the working face, or table. [20]The anvil has a long and pointed beak which is used for bending metal bars. [21]Rough work, such as cutting through metal with a chisel, is done on a step, or ledge, which is located between the beak and the table. [22]The hammering of red hot metal is done on the hardened table.

(h) The working face is made of hardened steel.
(i) Chiselling work is done either on a step or on a ledge.
(j) Red hot metal is hammered into shape on the working face.

[23]There are two holes in the working face. [24]The square hole, which is called the hardie hole, is used for putting the square shanks of bottom tools, such as the hardie and fuller, in position. [25]The small round hole called the punch hole, or pritchel, is used for two purposes. [26]It can support round bars during forging operations such as upsetting, and it provides clearance for punches when making holes in hot metal.

(k) There is a square hole on the anvil face, called the hardie hole, which is used for positioning hardies.
(l) The pritchel is where round bars can be supported while they are being upset.

Solutions

(a) Forging is a process . . . (1)
It (i.e. the process) consists of heating metal and pressing or hammering it into shape. (2)
i.e. Forging is a process which consists of heating metal and pressing or hammering it into shape.
= *Forging is a process in which metal is heated and pressed or hammered into shape.*

(b) Both ferrous and non-ferrous metals may be forged. (3)
i.e. SOME metals in both classes of metals, ferrous and non-ferrous, may be forged.
≠ ALL metals in both classes of metals, ferrous and non-ferrous, may be forged.
≠ All ferrous and non-ferrous metals may be forged.
i.e. It is NOT TRUE to say that all ferrous and non-ferrous metals may be forged.

(c) Both ferrous and non-ferrous metals may be forged, but it is usually the former that are forged by hand processes. (3)

it is usually the former = it is usually ferrous metals

i.e. it is usually, but not always, the case that ferrous metals are forged . . .

i.e. Some non-ferrous metals may be forged by hand processes, too.

∴ Not only ferrous metals are forged by hand processes but non-ferrous metals are forged by hand processes, too.

∴ It is NOT TRUE to say that only ferrous metals are forged by hand processes.

(d) The most suitable metal for this purpose is wrought iron. (4)

the most suitable metal = the best metal

this purpose i.e. forging by hand processes (3)

Wrought iron is a ferrous metal. (see Unit 4.)

∴ The best ferrous metal for hand forging is wrought iron.

= *Wrought iron is the best ferrous metal for hand forging.*

(e) Modern forging hearths are made of plates of cast iron or steel. (5)

= A modern forging hearth is made of . . . either cast iron or steel.

i.e. 2 names, 2 things

c.f. . . . modern forges, or forging hearths, . . .⎫
. . . the working face, or table, . . .   ⎬ 2 names, 1 thing
. . . a step, or ledge, . . .   ⎭

(Compare Unit 1, sentence 2 with Unit 1 sentences 5, 6)

plates of cast iron or steel = cast iron plates or steel plates = cast iron or steel plates

∴ *A modern forging hearth is made of either cast iron or steel plates.*

(f) Above the fire-place is a flue . . . (8)

= A flue is above the fire-place.

= There is a flue above the fire-place.

Its purpose is to carry away the fumes from the fire. (9)

i.e. The purpose of the flue above the fire-place is to carry away . . .

[We can express a purpose simply by using a *to+infinitive* (see Unit 3, Grammar Exercise A).]

∴ There is a flue above the fire-place. Its purpose is to carry away the fumes from the fire.

= *There is a flue above the fire-place to carry away the fumes.*

(g) Behind the heart is a blower which is driven by electric power. (10)

= Behind the hearth is a power-driven blower.

It (i.e. the blower) is connected to the tuyere through which a draught of air is blown into the fire. (11)

through which a draught of air is blown = which blows a draught of air through the tuyere . . .

i.e. *A power-driven blower blows a draught of air through the tuyere into the fire.*

(h) . . . on a surface which is made of hardened steel. (18)
This surface is known as the working face. (19)
i.e. *The working face is made of hardened steel.*

(i) Rough work, such as cutting through metal with a chisel, is done on a step, or ledge. (21)
cutting through metal with a chisel = chiselling work
a step, or ledge, i.e. 1 thing, 2 names (see **(e)** above)
∴ EITHER Chiselling work is done on a step.
  OR Chiselling work is done on a ledge.
  BUT NOT Chiselling work is done either on a step or on a ledge.

(j) The hammering of red hot metal is done on the hardened table. (22)
the hardened table = the working face (19)
The hammering of red hot metal is done on the table.
= Red hot metal is hammered on the table.
i.e. *Red hot metal is hammered into shape on the working face.*

(k) There are two holes in the working face. (23) . . . a square hole, which is called the hardie hole . . . (24)
= There is a square hole on the anvil face, called the hardie hole.
(The hardie hole) is used for putting the square shanks of bottom tools, such as the hardie and the fuller, in position. (24)
putting . . . in position = positioning
i.e. The hardie hole is used for positioning bottom tools, such as the hardie and the fuller.
bottom tools such as the hardie and the fuller i.e. hardies and fullers and other bottom tools, e.g. chisels, swages.
∴ *There is a square hole on the anvil face, called the hardie hole which is used for positioning hardies (and fullers and bottom chisels etc.)*

(l) It (i.e. the punch hole, or pritchel) can be used for supporting round bars during forging operations such as upsetting. (26)
∴ The pritchel is where round bars can be supported . . .
during forging operations such as upsetting = while (round bars) are being upset
∴ *The pritchel is where round bars can be supported while they are being upset.*

EXERCISE A *Contextual reference*

1. In sentence 2 the first *it* refers to:
   (a) a smithy
   (b) forging
2. In sentence 4 *this purpose* refers to:
   (a) heating metal
   (b) forging by hand
   (c) pressing into shape
3. In sentence 9 *its* refers to:
   (a) the chimney's
   (b) the hood's
   (c) the flue's
4. In sentence 12 *it* refers to:
   (a) the draught of air
   (b) the fire
   (c) the tuyere
5. In sentence 13 *it* refers to:
   (a) the draught of air
   (b) the tuyere

EXERCISE B *Rephrasing*

Rewrite the following, using words and constructions from the text to replace those printed in italics. For examples, see Unit 1, Exercise B.
1. It is usually ferrous metals that are forged by *operations which are done by hand.*
2. The *plates of steel* of a forging hearth may be *joined together with rivets.*
3. Located behind the forging hearth is the *tank of water for cooling the draught of air which is blown through the fire.*
4. The surface on which hot metal is shaped is called the *table.*
5. *The small round hole on the anvil face* can be used for *holding up* round metal bars during forging.

EXERCISE C *Relationships between statements*

Place the following words or phrases in the sentences indicated. Replace, re-order and add to the words in the sentences where necessary. For examples, see Unit 1, Exercise C.

(a) may be defined as (2)	(d) therefore (13)
(b) although (3)	(e) thus (15)
(c) because (12)	

EXERCISE D *Restatements*

Restate information given in the reading passage by omitting or replacing words in the sentences indicated below.

EXAMPLE

Sentence 6: Those which are made of cast iron are bolted together, whereas those which are made of steel are riveted or welded together.

= Those made of cast iron are bolted together, whereas those made of steel are riveted or welded together.

(a) 7   (b) 8   (c) 10   (d) 13   (e) 15   (f) 18 (2 clauses)   (g) 20   (h) 21   (i) 24

EXERCISE E *Labelling of diagrams*

Draw these diagrams and label your drawings with the words listed below.

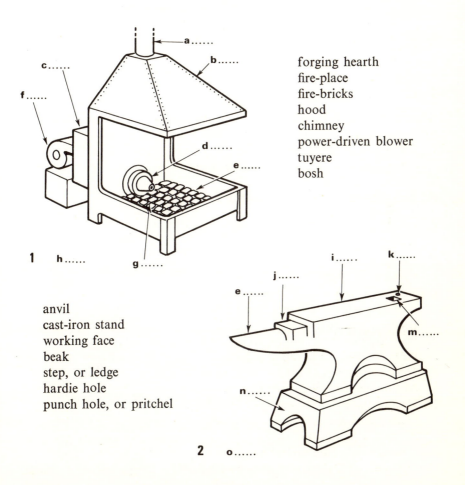

forging hearth
fire-place
fire-bricks
hood
chimney
power-driven blower
tuyere
bosh

anvil
cast-iron stand
working face
beak
step, or ledge
hardie hole
punch hole, or pritchel

EXERCISE F *Inductions, deductions and predictions: the properties of metals*

We can perform certain tests on metals to show whether they are malleable, or brittle, or ductile etc.

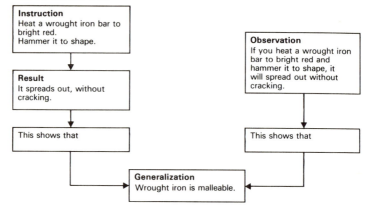

A GENERALIZATION made on the basis of an OBSERVATION is known as an INDUCTION.

Part 1

Arrange the information below in the same way as in the diagram above. In this way you will make generalizations which are inductions.

(a) Pull a copper rod through a die.
   It lengthens into a wire, without cracking.
   Copper is ductile.

(b) Rub the surface of a tool steel bar with a fine file.
   It leaves no mark on the bar.
   High carbon steel is hard.

(c) Hit a $\frac{3}{8}''$ diam. cast iron bar with a 1 lb hammer.
   It snaps easily.
   Cast iron is brittle.

(d) Heat a bar of lead to melting point.
   It melts readily at a low temperature.
   Lead is a fusible metal.

(e) Place an aluminium rod on a piece of heat-sensitive paper.
   Place one end of the rod in a flame.
   The paper alongside the rod turns green quickly.
   Aluminium is a good thermal conductor.

(f) Hacksaw one-third of the way through a mild steel bar.
   Place it in a vice.
   Strike it with a hammer.
   It breaks only after several blows.
   Mild steel is tough and can absorb a great deal of energy before it fractures.

(g) Put a bronze plate on two parallel steel bars.
Place a heavy load on the plate between the bars.
The bronze plate bends slightly.
Remove the load.
The plate returns to its original shape.
Bronze is elastic.

Part 2

In Part 1 you practised one form of expressing observations, as in (i) below. Other ways of expressing observations are given in (ii), (iii) and (iv). Study these carefully.

(i) If you heat a wrought iron bar to bright red and hammer it to shape, it will spread out without cracking.

(ii) If a wrought iron bar *is heated* to bright red and *hammered* to shape, it will spread out without cracking.

(iii) If a wrought iron bar is heated to bright red and hammered to shape, it *spreads* out without cracking.

(iv) *When* a wrought iron bar is heated to bright red and hammered to shape, it spreads out without cracking.

Now express the observations in the inductions which you have made in Part 1 above in different ways.

Part 3

In Part 1 the induction (i.e. the generalization which was based on an observation) was introduced by the words *This shows that* ... In the following table, five other ways of introducing an induction are given. Study them carefully.

Observation		Generalization
If you heat a wrought iron bar to bright red and hammer it to shape, it will spread without cracking.	This shows that Thus, Hence, Therefore, This demonstrates that This indicates that	Wrought iron is malleable.

Now express some of the observations and inductions of Parts 1 and 2, using *thus, hence,* etc.

Part 4

When we make a generalization first and relate it to an observation, we call this a DEDUCTION.

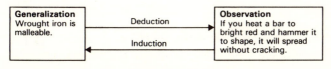

Generalization		Observation
Wrought iron is malleable.	Deduction → ← Induction	If you heat a bar to bright red and hammer it to shape, it will spread without cracking.

Change the inductions you have made in Parts 1, 2, and 3 above into deductions by using the terms *thus, therefore, hence,* and *consequently*. Do *not* use the expressions: *This shows that, This demonstrates that* or *This indicates that.*

EXAMPLE

Wrought iron is malleable. Thus (therefore, hence, consequently), if you heat a bar to bright red and hammer it to shape, it will spread out without cracking.

Part 5

Study the following statements:

(i) Wrought iron is malleable and ductile. (ii) For example, if a wrought iron bar is heated to bright red and hammered to shape, it will spread out without cracking.

(i) is a generalization. (ii) is an observation which is used as an EXAMPLE.

Observations which follow generalizations are often used as examples.
Change the deductions you have made in Part 4 above into generalizations +examples.

Part 6

Instead of saying *Wrought iron is malleable*, we can say *Wrought iron has the property of malleability.*
Express the generalizations you have made in Part 1 above, using these words:

ductility, fusibility, thermal conductivity, elasticity, hardness,
brittleness, toughness.

Part 7

We may define the properties of metals on the basis of their observable characteristics.
(a) From the table below, choose the observable characteristics in column B which define the properties listed in column A. Write out full definitions using the pattern:
A *is the property which enables a metal to* B.

EXAMPLE

Malleability is the property which enables a metal to be shaped by hammering without cracking. (Note the use of the passive.)

A PROPERTY	B OBSERVABLE CHARACTERISTICS
1. Malleability	(a) breaks easily when hit with a hammer.
2. Ductility	(b) absorbs a great deal of energy without fracturing.
3. Fusibility	(c) conducts heat or electricity.
4. Conductivity	(d) is shaped by hammering without cracking.
5. Elasticity	(e) melts readily at a low temperature.
6. Hardness	(f) is drawn out into a wire without cracking.
7. Toughness	(g) returns to its original shape after a heavy load has been removed.
8. Brittleness	(h) resists scratching, wear and abrasion.

(b) Another way of stating the property of a metal is as follows:

A metal which breaks easily when hit with a hammer possesses the property of brittleness.

Write statements in this way using the table above.

Part 8

A definition+a generalization may be followed by an observation which is also a PREDICTION. A prediction is a statement of result about what *will* happen (i.e. in the future) if something is done.

EXAMPLE

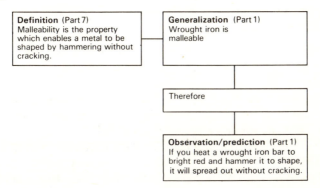

The contents of this diagram can be written out as a paragraph, as follows:
Malleability is the property which enables a metal to be shaped by hammering without cracking. Wrought iron is malleable; therefore, if you heat a wrought iron bar to bright red and hammer it to shape, it will spread out without cracking.

Write out short paragraphs, as in the example above, which consist of a definition from Part 7 above, followed by a generalization from Part 1 above, and an observation/prediction also from Part 1. The following information will help you:

	DEFINITION	GENERALIZATION	OBSERVATION/PREDICTION
(a)	ductility	copper	pull through a die
(b)	fusibility	lead	heat to melting point
(c)	conductivity	aluminium	place on heat-sensitive paper
(d)	elasticity	bronze	heavy load placed on plate
(e)	hardness	tool steel	scratched with a fine file
(f)	toughness	mild steel	hacksawed, and struck
(g)	brittleness	cast iron	hit with a hammer

II   GRAMMAR

EXERCISE A *Relative clauses introduced by a preposition*

A common type of relative clause in technical English has a preposition before *which*. Such clauses are formed in the following way.

EXAMPLE
   Some metals are called non-ferrous metals.
   The basic material *in these metals is* not iron.
   = Metals *in which* the basic material is not iron are called non-ferrous metals.

Join the following pairs of sentences together to form one sentence so that they contain relative clauses beginning with a *preposition+which*, as in the example above.
1. Forging is a process. In this process heated metal is shaped by hammering.
2. A vice consists of a cast iron or steel body. Into the body is fitted a square section insert shaped into a jaw at its outer end.
3. The majority of materials are metallic. An engineer has to deal with such materials.
4. The edges of a swage block have a series of grooves. Heavy work can be swaged on these grooves.
5. Welding is a joining process. A small area of the parent metal is melted in this process and allowed to solidify.
6. Grey iron is the principal material. Iron castings are made from this material.
7. Pig iron is the raw material. Cast irons and steels are made from it.

8. The temperature is about 1300°C. Wrought iron may be successfully welded at this temperature.

EXERCISE B *Noun+noun constructions*

An adjective is often used to modify a noun. For example:

ferrous metal	*adjustable* frame
cast iron	*heavy*, *rigid* bench
stainless steel	*red-hot* metal

A noun may also be used to modify another noun. Many different kinds of relationship are possible in such *noun+noun* constructions. Study the following carefully:

A *with* B:	calipers with a spring = spring calipers
A *contains* B:	an alloy which contains nickel = a nickel alloy
A *of* B:	the base of a machine = the machine base
A *for* B:	a tank for water = a water tank
A *used for* B-*ing*:	a hole used for punching metal = a punch hole
A *made from* B:	a brush made from wire = a wire brush
A *which uses* B:	a forge which uses coke = a coke forge
A *shaped like* B:	a magnet shaped like a horseshoe = a horseshoe magnet
A {*operated*/*done*} *by* B:	a file operated by hand = a hand file

Notice that we can write a simple definition of each noun+noun compound by means of a statement which makes the relationship between the nouns clear.

EXAMPLES

Spring calipers are calipers with (=which have) a spring attached.
A nickel alloy is an alloy which contains nickel as an important element.
A punch hole on an anvil is the hole which is used for punching metal.
A coke forge is a forging hearth which uses coke as fuel.

Now write statements which show the full meaning of the following noun +noun compounds. If possible write statements which are definitions of the object.

1. aluminium alloy	7. pick-up tongs	14. a hacksaw blade
2. a spring swage	8. hand forging	15. a gear box
3. a surface table	9. marking-out tools	16. a gas cylinder
4. high-speed steel	10. wire bristles	17. manganese bronze
5. a diamond-point chisel	11. asbestos gloves	18. vernier calipers
6. a conveyor belt	12. overall buttons	19. a surface plate
	13. a motor vehicle	20. a locking nut

21. heat treatment	31. a leather apron	41. a power hacksaw
22. screw threads	32. wing nuts	42. a steel rule
23. a hammer head	33. a metal bar	43. press tools
24. a machine bed	34. a quenching tank	44. silver soldering
25. a depth gauge	35. a metal joint	45. phosphor bronze
26. machine tools	36. a sand mould	46. sheet steel
27. a cast iron stand	37. steel plates	47. power tools
28. wheel diameter	38. a petrol tank	48. a star wheel
29. vee blocks	39. water pipes	49. air pipes
30. a hardie hole	40. the drive motor	50. bar solder

The following are more difficult:

51. pipe cutter	54. drill chuck guard
52. gas regulator	55. a lathe operator
53. tool holder	

EXERCISE C *Participle+noun constructions*

Apart from *adjective+noun* and *noun+noun* phrases, there are a large number of modifiers which are made up of a *verb stem+suffix*. Two important classes of modifiers are as follows:

(i) Modifiers formed from verbs by adding *-ing* (present participles). These modifiers are usually active in meaning.

EXAMPLES
cutting tools = tools which cut (something).
drilling machine = a machine which drills (something).

(ii) Modifiers formed from verbs by using the past participle form (e.g. lubricated, made, known etc.). These modifiers are usually passive in meaning.

EXAMPLES
a lubricated bearing = a bearing which has been lubricated.
compressed air = air which has been compressed.

Now write down and complete the sentences by filling in the blanks with a past participle modifier or a present participle modifier. Form each modifier from one of the verbs in this list.

temper	shape	strike	season	cut	drive
fit	compress	scribe	harden (2)	ventilate	grind
operate	machine	move	measure	lock	

1. A line parallel to a straight edge can be drawn with a . . . block.
2. Vee blocks can be made from cast iron or . . . steel.
3. A . . . ring should be placed on the handles of the tongs during a long . . . job.

4. A well . . . forge is essential as the fumes given off from a coke fire are poisonous.
5. It is important that correctly . . . tongs are used to lift metal from fire to anvil. For example, round-mouth tongs should be used to lift a metal bar at its end.
6. A hammer consists of a head and a shaft. The head is made from cast steel with a . . . pein and . . . face, and the shaft is usually made from well . . . wood.
7. A chisel's blunt . . . edge should be sharpened on an off-hand . . . machine.
8. Hand . . . bench shears may be used for cutting sheet metal.
9. A power . . . hacksaw is used for the rough cutting of metal bars.
10. Lathes are used for . . . processes when the work can be turned and cut with a tool.
11. It is important that an overall with closely . . . sleeves should be worn in the workshop.
12. Ties and scarves should not be worn as they can get caught in . . . machinery.
13. . . . instruments like micrometers and vernier calipers should be kept in boxes in order to prevent dust and rust forming on the instruments.

EXERCISE D *Complex noun phrases*

The noun phrases in Exercise C can be made even more complex by the addition of more nouns, adjectives and participles.

EXAMPLES
   (i) A hacksaw blade which is flexible
  = A flexible hacksaw blade
  (ii) Steel plates which are riveted together
  = Riveted steel plates
 (iii) A hammer head which is made of steel which has been hardened . . .
  = A hardened steel hammer head
 (iv) Asbestos sheets which are proof against fire
  = Fire-proof asbestos sheets

Notice that each modifier we add sub-classifies the object that we are naming. Thus, in technical English, we can be very precise about an object (e.g. a part of a machine) by labelling it according to:

(a) its specific properties or qualities ((i) above)
(b) how it is made or constructed ((ii) above)
(c) what it is made from ((iii) above)
(d) its function or use, which may depend on its properties ((iv) above).

Rewrite the following sentences by moving information from the relative clause to make the noun phrases in italics more complex.

EXAMPLE
>   *A hacksaw* which is driven by power is used for the rough cutting of metal bars and strips.
> = *A power driven hacksaw* is used for the rough cutting of metal bars and strips.

(Note that compound words like *power driven* are often printed with a hyphen: power-driven)

1. *Guillotines* which are operated by power can cut sheet steel to the correct length and width.
2. The capstan lathe is so called because of the *tool carrier* which is shaped like a hexagon.
3. *Power tools* which are held in the hand must be properly earthed.
4. *Welding* which is done by an electric arc is extremely efficient as the temperature of the spark between the two terminals of the electric circuit is approximately 3300°C.
5. *The electrode*, which is coated with a flux, itself provides the filler metal.
6. A *bending machine* which is of the roller type may be used for forming flat sheets into cylindrical shapes.
7. Behind the forge there are *valves* which regulate the blast entering through the tuyere and which control the temperature of the fire.
8. *Cylinder blocks* which are for motor vehicles are usually made of cast iron although some are now made of aluminium.
9. The *working face* of an anvil, which is made of cast steel and has been hardened, is where red hot metal is hammered into shape by the blacksmith.
10. A *bar* which is made of mild steel and which has been hardened by work can be restored to its original condition by the process of annealing.
11. *Cylinders* which contain air which is compressed are coloured grey and have a right hand thread, whereas *cylinders* which contain acetylene gas which is inflammable have a left hand thread and are coloured maroon.
12. *Cutting tools* which are made of high speed steel have great strength and toughness and can be used at high temperatures.

6 Heat treatment

[1]A carbon steel bar will become hard and brittle if it is struck repeatedly when being worked. [2]A metal which has become work-hardened in this way can be made softer and more workable again. [3]The process of doing this is called annealing. [4]It restores the metal to its original and natural condition. [5]The process consists of heating the metal to the correct annealing temperature and allowing it to cool slowly in sand. [6]For low carbon steel the necessary annealing temperature is about 900°C. [7]Great care should be taken not to overheat the metal.

(a) Work-hardened metals can be annealed to make them softer and more workable.
(b) The result of striking a carbon-steel bar repeatedly is that it becomes work-hardened.

[8]A chisel needs to be hard in order to cut other softer metals. [9]So it has to be hardened. [10]This process consists of heating the chisel to a cherry red colour. [11]After that, it is plunged vertically into cold water, and moved about rapidly. [12]This prevents cracking. [13]This operation is called quenching. [14]It makes the steel very hard, but brittle.

(c) The operation of plunging a steel bar into cold water after it has been heated is called quenching.
(d) A chisel must be hardened so as to cut other softer metals.
(e) The hardening process makes a steel bar brittle.

[15]Brittleness may be reduced by tempering. [16]The part which is to be tempered is first cleaned. [17]The metal is heated and the different colours which appear on the metal noted. [18]These are called temper colours. [19]The first one to appear is yellow. [20]This is followed by brown, and finally blue. [21]The right colour for a chisel is purple. [22]When this colour is reached, it

should be immediately quenched in water. [23]The chisel is hard, but now less brittle.

(f) When the metal is heated, the first temper colour which appears is yellow.

(g) A chisel which has been tempered is not suitable for cutting work.

Solutions

(a)   A metal which has become work-hardened in this way can be made softer and more workable again. (2)

=   A work-hardened metal can be made softer and more workable again. The process of doing this is called annealing. (3)

i.e.   The process of making a metal softer and more workable again is called annealing.

∴   A work-hardened metal can be annealed to make it softer and more workable.

=   *Work-hardened metals can be annealed to make them softer and more workable.*

(b)   A carbon steel bar will become hard and brittle if it is struck repeatedly when being worked. (1)

=   A carbon steel bar will become work-hardened if it is struck repeatedly during work.

=   If a carbon steel bar is struck repeatedly, it will become work-hardened.

=   *The result of striking a carbon steel bar repeatedly is that it becomes work-hardened.*

(c)   After that (i.e. heating the chisel to a cherry red colour (10)) it is plunged . . . into cold water. (11) . . . This operation is called quenching. (13)

i.e.   *The operation of plunging a steel bar into cold water after it has been heated is called quenching.*

(d)   A chisel needs to be hard in order to cut other softer metals. (8) A chisel needs to be hard ∴ it has to be hardened (9) = it must be hardened.

i.e.   A chisel must be hardened in order to cut other softer metals.

=   *A chisel must be hardened so as to cut other softer metals.*

(e)   A chisel . . . has to be hardened. (8+9) (see **(e)** above) This process consists of heating the chisel. (10) After that, . . . it is quenched. (11–13)

This process refers to hardening = the hardening process i.e. heating and quenching.

It (i.e. the hardening process) makes the steel very hard, but brittle. (14)

i.e.   *The hardening process makes a steel bar brittle.*

(f) These (i.e. the different colours which appear on the metal) are called temper colours. (18)

The first one to appear is yellow. (19)

The first one to appear = The first temper colour which appears.

∴ *When the metal is heated, the first temper colour which appears is yellow.*

(g) (Hardening and quenching) makes the steel very hard, but brittle. (14)

i.e. It is not suitable for cutting work because it is brittle.

Brittleness may be reduced by tempering. (16)

The chisel is hard, but now less brittle. (23)

∴ A chisel which has been tempered is suitable for cutting work (because it is less brittle than before).

i.e. It is NOT TRUE to say that a chisel which has been tempered is not suitable for cutting work.

EXERCISE A *Contextual reference*

1. In sentence 3, *this* refers to:
   (a) making a metal softer and more workable
   (b) work-hardening
   (c) striking a mild steel bar repeatedly
2. In sentence 4, *it* refers to:
   (a) work-hardening
   (b) the process of annealing
3. In sentence 10, *this process* refers to:
   (a) annealing
   (b) cutting softer metal
   (c) hardening
4. In sentence 12, *this* refers to:
   (a) plunging the chisel vertically into cold water
   (b) moving the chisel about rapidly
   (c) plunging the chisel into cold water and moving it about rapidly
5. In sentence 14, *it* refers to:
   (a) quenching
   (b) cracking
   (c) hardening
6. In sentence 22, *it* refers to:
   (a) the right colour
   (b) the chisel

EXERCISE B *Rephrasing*

Rewrite the following, using words and constructions from the text to replace those printed in italics. For examples, see Unit 1.

1. A chisel is *plunged vertically into cold water and moved about* after it has been heated to a cherry red colour.

2. *The process of making a metal softer and more workable changes* a metal back to *the condition it was before it became hardened.*
3. Annealing can be performed on a carbon steel bar which has become *hard and brittle during work.*
4. It is important that steel which is being annealed should not be *made too hot.*
5. *The property which causes a metal to break easily* can be reduced by *heating the metal to its correct temper colour and quenching it.*

EXERCISE C *Relationships between statements*

Place the following words or phrases in the sentences indicated. Replace and re-order the words in the sentences where necessary. For examples, see Unit 1, Exercise C.

(a) however (2)   (e) in order to (11 + 12)
(b) the name of the process for . . . (3)   (f) as a result . . . (14)
(c) however (7)   (g) then (17)
(d) therefore (9)   (h) it will be found that (23)

EXERCISE D *Description of an operation and its result*

Study the following:

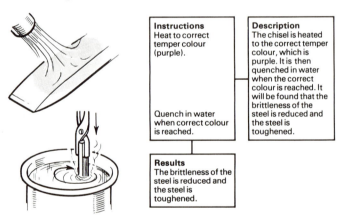

Instructions	Description
Heat to correct temper colour (purple).	The chisel is heated to the correct temper colour, which is purple. It is then quenched in water when the correct colour is reached. It will be found that the brittleness of the steel is reduced and the steel is toughened.
Quench in water when correct colour is reached.	

Results
The brittleness of the steel is reduced and the steel is toughened.

Note: in INSTRUCTIONS (i) the imperative form of the verb is used, and (ii) definite and indefinite articles before nouns are omitted.

Part 1

Below you will see six sets of diagrams (a) to (f), and two lists, A and B. From the instructions in list A choose those which tell you how to perform the operations illustrated in the diagrams. Choose a statement of result from list B. Then write out a description of the process, as shown in the example above.

(a) Annealing a work-hardened steel bar:

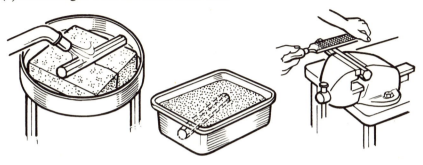

(b) Carburizing, or case hardening, a mild steel component:

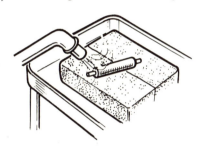 

(c) Hardening a chisel:

(d) Normalizing a metal component:

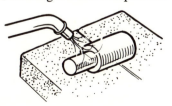 

(e) Upsetting a metal bar:

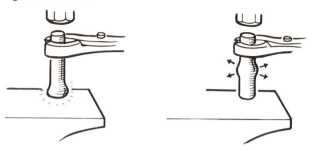

(f) Drawing down a metal bar:

 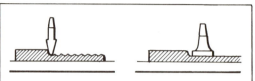

LIST A
Instructions

1. Heat to bright red.
   Dip in carbon rich mixture.
   Repeat process to ensure sufficient carbon intake.
2. Heat bar at part to be upset.
   Strike end of bar with hammer.
3. Heat bar to dull red.
   Allow to cool slowly in sand or ashes.
   Test with a file.
4. Heat bar at point to be drawn down.
   Increase length of bar by using a fuller.
   Finish with a flatter.
5. Heat chisel to cherry red.
   Plunge vertically into cold water.
   Move about rapidly to prevent cracking.
6. Heat component to same temperature as for hardening.
   Leave to cool freely in draught-free air.

LIST B
Results

i. The component absorbs carbon into its surface layer, which makes it very hard when suitably heat treated.
ii. This makes the chisel very hard, but brittle.
iii. This increases the length of the bar but decreases the width and thickness.
iv. This restores the metal's malleability, which makes it workable again.

v. This increases the thickness of the metal bar at the expense of its length.

vi. Stresses set up in the metal during cold working are removed and the metal is returned to its normal condition.

Part 2 Compare your answers in 1 above to those in Unit 5, Exercise F, Parts 2, 3 and 4.

INSTRUCTIONS + STATEMENTS OF RESULT can be changed into OBSERVATIONS and DESCRIPTIONS.

The writer chooses one of these forms of expression according to his purpose.

(i) INSTRUCTIONS + STATEMENTS OF RESULT are used when the writer wants to tell the reader how to carry out an operation. For example:

Heat wrought iron bar to bright red. Hammer to shape. It spreads out without cracking. (Unit 5, Exercise F)

(ii) DESCRIPTIONS are also used when the writer wants to tell the reader how to carry out an operation. For example:

A wrought iron bar is heated to bright red and hammered to shape. It will be found that the bar will spread out without cracking.

(iii) OBSERVATIONS are used when the writer wants to refer to the results of an operation in order to make a deduction or induction, or in order to illustrate a generalization. For example:

If a wrought iron bar is heated to bright red and hammered to shape, it will spread out without cracking. This shows that wrought iron is malleable. (Unit 5, Exercise F)

(i), (ii) and (iii) all contain the same information. The difference between them is that they express the information in different ways. They are different kinds of communication.

Part 3 Write out the observations from Exercise F, Part 1 in Unit 5 as descriptions.

EXAMPLE

A wrought iron bar is heated to bright red and hammered to shape. It will be found that the bar will spread out without cracking.

OR It will be found that the bar can be spread out without cracking.

Part 4 In Part 1 above, the aim, or purpose, of the operation is expressed in the heading above the illustrations, e.g. *hardening a chisel, annealing a work-hardened steel bar* etc. A description of an operation can be preceded by a statement of the aim, or purpose, of doing it. (see Unit 3, Grammar)

EXAMPLE

To temper a chisel it is first heated to the correct temper colour, which is purple, and then quenched in water. This reduces the brittleness and toughens the steel.

1. Write out the descriptions in Part 1 in this way. Above each description

write a statement of purpose. Use words like *first, then* and *finally* to introduce each stage of the process.

2. Now write out the descriptions you have written in Part 3 above, in the same way. Note that the statement of purpose is taken from the generalizations which follow the observations in Exercise F, Unit 5. *This shows that = To show that*; *This demonstrates that = To demonstrate that . . .*

EXAMPLE

To show that wrought iron is malleable, a wrought iron bar is first heated to bright red and then hammered to shape. It will be found that the bar can spread out without cracking.

Part 5 Write out the descriptions in Part 1 above as observations. Write generalizations about the heat treatment process, for (a), (b) and (d). For (c), (e) and (f) write defining statements beginning 'This process is called . . .'

EXAMPLE

If a chisel is heated to a purple colour and quenched in water when this colour is reached, the brittleness of the steel is reduced. Thus, tempering softens the metal but makes it much tougher.

EXERCISE E *Instructions based on descriptions*

Part 1 Study the following description carefully.

Drawing down a circular bar to a square taper

A black mild steel bar of particular dimensions has to be drawn down to a square taper. The tools required are anvil, tongs and ball-pein hammer. Throughout the operation the end which is being forged must be kept at a bright red heat. The procedure is as follows. The circular bar is gripped with the tongs. One face is forged flat and to a short taper. The component is rotated through 180° and the opposite face is forged flat and to a short taper. The work is turned through 90° and the above operation is repeated. The end is drawn down to the required length. It is important to keep the faces square during the operations. The result is a circular bar with a square taper at one end.

The above description can also be expressed as a set of instructions on an operations sheet (or work-sheet), like the one given below. On the operations sheet the information is changed in a number of ways, as follows:

1. The title of the description is changed from *Drawing down . . .* to *To draw down . . .*
2. In the description the purpose of the operation is repeated at the end as a statement of its result. In the instructions it is not necessary to state the result, because this is clearly seen in the diagrams.
3. In instructions we often omit
   (i) the definite and the indefinite articles (i.e. *the, a, an*)
   (ii) relative pronouns (i.e. *which, that*)
   (iii) some parts of the verb *to be* (i.e. *is, are*)

We use only those words which are necessary to give the essential information, as in a telegram.

Now write out and complete the operations sheet, giving only essential instructions based on the description above.

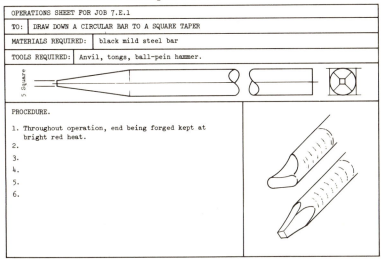

OPERATIONS SHEET FOR JOB 7.E.1	
TO:	DRAW DOWN A CIRCULAR BAR TO A SQUARE TAPER
MATERIALS REQUIRED:	black mild steel bar
TOOLS REQUIRED:	Anvil, tongs, ball-pein hammer.

PROCEDURE.

1. Throughout operation, end being forged kept at bright red heat.
2.
3.
4.
5.
6.

Part 2 Write out operations sheets for each of the following descriptions.

1. A black mild steel square bar has to be drawn down to a circular taper. The tools required are an anvil, vee-bit tongs and a ball-pein hammer. The end which is being forged must be kept at a bright red heat throughout the operation. The procedure is as follows. One end of the square bar is forged to a square taper. The work is placed on the anvil face so that a corner of the tapered portion is touching the anvil and the faces of the tapered portion are at 45° to the top of the anvil. The opposite faces are forged to produce an octagonal pyramid shape. All corners of the bar are lightly hammered to produce a conical taper. The result is a square bar drawn down to a circular taper, having a conical shape.

2. In order to manufacture a cold chisel a one piece octagonal bar of 0·8% high carbon steel is required. The tools required are an anvil, a ball-pein hammer, tongs, a quenching bath and an off-hand grinding machine. Throughout the operation the bar is heated to a bright red. The procedure is as follows. The bar is held at a slight angle on the anvil face. One face is drawn down to form a wedge shape. The bar is turned through 180° and the opposite face is drawn down to a wedge shape. The bar is reversed and a chamfer is forged on the striking end. The bar is allowed to cool slowly and the cutting edge is roughly ground. The chisel is then hardened and tempered. Finally, the cutting edge is finish-ground on the grinding machine, and the cutting quality of the chisel tested on a mild steel block.

II GRAMMAR

EXERCISE A *Time expressions:* after, before, when, as soon as, while, until

Part 1 Look at these sentences:

(i) *First* the chisel is heated to a cherry red colour, *then* it is plunged vertically into water.
(ii) *After* the chisel is heated to a cherry red colour, it is plunged vertically into water.

Now rewrite the following sentences in the same way. Choose the appropriate time expression from the brackets and put it *at the beginning* of the sentence. Omit the words in italics.

1. A carbon steel bar has been struck repeatedly. *As a result* it becomes work-hardened. (when, before, after)
2. *At the exact moment* the temper colour reaches purple, the chisel is quenched in water. (while, as soon as, until)
3. A mild steel bar has been annealed. *Then* it is tested for workability with a file. (before, after, until)
4. The operations of hacksawing, chiselling and filing are performed in the fitting workshop, *but first* the metal has to be marked out accurately on a marking out table. (until, before, after)
5. The operation of drawing down is taking place. *During this process* the end which is being forged is kept at a bright red heat. (while, as soon as, until)
6. *Once* sheet metal has been marked out and cut to size, it *then* has to be formed into its final shape. (before, while, after)
7. A mild steel bar has been annealed. *As a result* it is restored to its original condition. (while, until, after)

8. A surface has been scraped by a scraper with strokes in one direction. *Afterwards* it must be scraped with strokes at 90° to the first ones. (when, before, while)
9. Metal is hardened. It can become brittle then. (as soon as, when, while)
10. *If* the wing nut at one end of a hacksaw is tightened, the tension of the blade is increased. (while, until, when)

Part 2 Look at this sentence:

(i) *After* the chisel has been heated to a cherry red colour, it is plunged into water.

We can state this in a negative form, as follows:

(ii) The chisel is *not* plunged into water *until* it has been heated to a cherry red colour.

Now look at the sentences you wrote in Part 1, and rewrite sentences 1–8 as in (ii) above, using *until*:

EXERCISE B *Time expressions:* then, during, throughout, prior to, first

Compare the following sentences with your answers to Exercise A, Part 1. If the sentences have approximately the same meaning put a tick after your written sentence; if not, put a cross. The first two sentences have been done for you.
1. A mild steel bar becomes work hardened and then it is struck repeatedly.   ✕
2. The temper colour should be purple before the chisel is quenched in water.   √
3. During the process of annealing a mild steel bar is tested for workability with a file.
4. The metal is marked out accurately on the marking out table, then the operations of hacksawing, chiselling and filing are performed.
5. Throughout the operation of drawing down the end being forged is maintained at a bright red heat.
6. Sheet metal has to be formed into its final shape prior to marking out and cutting to size.
7. A mild steel bar has been restored to its original condition through the process of annealing.
8. First, we use a surface grinder to produce a smooth surface, then we use a power hacksaw to rough cut the metal bar.
9. A surface is scraped by a scraper with strokes in one direction and prior to it being scraped with strokes at 90° to the first ones.
10. Metal sometimes becomes brittle if it is hardened.
11. The wing nut at one end of a hacksaw is tightened as a result of the tension of the blade being increased.
12. If a drilling machine is running, the gear lever should not be moved.

EXERCISE C *Short-form time clauses*

(i) *After a mild steel bar is annealed*, it regains its original properties.
   (=*After a mild steel bar has been annealed*, it regains . . .)
(ii) *After it is annealed*, a mild steel bar regains its original properties.
   (=*After it has been annealed*, a mild steel bar regains . . .)

These time clauses may be shortened as follows:

After being annealed, a mild steel bar regains its original properties.

Note also the following:

$\left.\begin{array}{l}\text{Before}\\ \text{Prior to}\end{array}\right\}$ being heated, the metal is cleaned with emery cloth.

$\left.\begin{array}{l}\text{While}\\ \text{When}\\ \text{On}\end{array}\right\}$ being hardened, metal sometimes becomes brittle.

Rewrite the sentences below, changing each time clause to a shortened form.

1. After the metal is heated to dull red, it is allowed to cool slowly in sand.
2. After the mild steel bar is hacksawed ⅓ of the way through, it is placed in a vice and struck with a hammer until it breaks.
3. Before we start to cut a thread with a tap, we must drill the right size of hole depending on the root diameter of the thread.
4. While the end of the metal bar is drawn down, it should be kept at a bright red heat.
5. After a mild steel bar has been kept at high temperatures for forging purposes, its structure can be refined by normalizing.
6. When calipers measure the diameter of a round bar, they should just touch the bar as they are passed over it.
7. When a wrought iron bar is hammered to shape, it spreads out without cracking. (Begin: 'On . . .')
8. Before sheet metal is bent and pressed, it is marked out and cut to shape.

7 Sheet metal work

I READING WITH COMPREHENSION PROBLEMS

[1]Sheet metal must possess the property of malleability. [2]Once the material has been cut to shape, bending and pressing operations are performed on it. [3]It is very important that the metal does not crack during these operations.

(a) Once sheet metal has been cut to shape, it is bent and pressed.
(b) The two operations in sheet metal work are bending and pressing.
(c) The metal used in sheet metal work is malleable.

[4]There are three main types of sheet metal. [5]If an ingot of mild steel is rolled and pressed while it is white hot, hot-rolled sheet steel is produced. [6]A further process, known as cold-rolling, produces a surface which is brighter and which has a better finish. [7]Another kind of sheet steel is tin-plate. [8]This is mild steel sheet which has been cold-rolled and then plated with a thin layer of tin. [9]Iron or steel sheet can also be coated with zinc on each side. [10]This process is called galvanizing. [11]The material produced is known as galvanized sheet iron or steel. [12]Both tin and zinc protect iron and steel from rust. [13]Zinc gives a better protective coating for steel than tin does.

(d) Cold-rolling takes place after sheet metal has been hot-rolled.
(e) Cold-rolled sheet steel has a brighter, better-finished surface than hot-rolled sheet steel.
(f) Galvanized sheet steel has a coating of zinc on both sides.

[14]A sheet metal worker marks out metal while it is in a flat form. [15]For this operation a knowledge of geometry is required. [16]The three-dimensional finished shape of an object never looks the same as its shape when it is marked out on flat metal. (see diagram) [17]It is essential to calculate and mark off enough metal to allow for bending and folding. [18]If such bending allowances are not made, the metal will not be sufficient for the bending and folding operations. [19]A scriber is usually used for marking out. [20]Tin-plate

should not be scratched too deeply. [21]If it is, the protective coating may be removed.

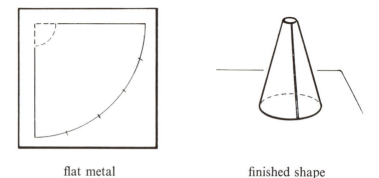

flat metal   finished shape

(g) Sufficient metal for bending and folding must be calculated and marked off.

(h) A sector of a circle is marked out on a flat sheet in the shape of a cone.

(i) Tin-plate is usually marked out with a scriber.

Solutions

(a) Once the material has been cut to shape, bending and pressing operations are performed on it. (2)

the material i.e. sheet metal (1)

bending and pressing operations = operations in which sheet metal is bent and pressed

∴ *Once sheet metal has been cut to shape, it is bent and pressed.*

(b) . . . bending and pressing operations are performed on it (i.e. sheet metal). (2)

∴ Bending and pressing are TWO operations in sheet metal work.
Cutting to shape is a third operation.

but the two operations = the ONLY two operations

∴ It is NOT TRUE to say that the (only) two operations in sheet metal work are bending and pressing.

(c) Sheet metal must possess the property of malleability. (1)

= Sheet metal must be malleable.

i.e. It is a necessary requirement that sheet metal is malleable (because) bending and pressing are performed on it. (2)

∴ *The metal used in sheet metal work is malleable.*

(d) If an ingot of mild steel is rolled and pressed while it is white hot, hot-rolled steel sheet is produced. (5)

A further process, known as cold-rolling . . . (6)
a further process i.e. a process which takes place AFTER hot-rolling
∴ Cold-rolling takes place after hot-rolling.
= *Cold-rolling takes place after sheet metal has been hot-rolled.*

(e) . . . cold-rolling produces a surface which is brighter and which has a better finish. (6)
i.e. Cold-rolling produces a surface which is brighter and which has a better finish than the surface of hot-rolled sheet steel. (5)
a surface which is brighter = a brighter surface
a surface which has a better finish = a better-finished surface
∴ Cold-rolling produces a brighter surface and a better-finished surface.
= Cold-rolling produces a brighter, better-finished surface.
i.e. *Cold-rolled sheet steel has a brighter, better-finished surface than hot-rolled sheet steel.*

(f) Steel sheet can also be coated with zinc on each side. (9)
steel sheet which is coated with zinc = steel sheet which has a coating of zinc
on each side = on both sides
This process is called galvanizing. (10) The material produced is known as galvanized sheet steel. (11)
∴ *Galvanized sheet steel has a coating of zinc on both sides.*

(g) It is essential to calculate and mark off enough metal to allow for bending and folding. (17)
= It is essential to calculate and mark off sufficient metal for bending and folding.
= *Sufficient metal for bending and folding must be calculated and marked off.*

(h) The curve in the flat metal shows a sector of a circle. The finished shape shows a cone. (see diagram)
∴ A cone is marked out on flat metal as a sector of a circle.
i.e. A sector of a circle is NOT marked out on a flat sheet in the shape of a cone.

(i) A scriber is usually used for marking out. (19)
∴ A scriber is usually used for marking out tin-plate.
= *Tin-plate is usually marked out with a scriber.*

EXERCISE A *Contextual reference*

1. In sentence 2, *it* refers to:
    (a) the material
    (b) sheet steel

2. In sentence 6, *a further process* refers to:
   (a) hot-rolling
   (b) cold-rolling
3. In sentence 8, *this* refers to:
   (a) sheet steel
   (b) tin-plate
4. In sentence 10, *this process* refers to:
   (a) coating with zinc
   (b) cold-rolling and plating with tin

EXERCISE B *Rephrasing*

Rewrite the following using words and constructions from the text to replace those printed in italics. For example, see Unit 1, Exercise B.
1. It is essential that the metal used in sheet metal work should have the property *which enables it to be drawn out or spread out.*
2. *Sheet steel which is rolled or pressed while it is white hot* can be cold-rolled to produce a brighter, better finish.
3. *Mild steel sheet which has been cold-rolled and then plated with a thin layer of tin* can be marked out with a scriber.
4. *Sheet steel which has a coating of zinc on each side* is protected from rust by the zinc coating.
5. *A man who works with sheet metal* must have a knowledge of geometry.
6. It is essential that *sufficient metal for bending and folding* should be calculated and marked off.
7. If tin-plate is scratched too deeply with a scriber during marking-out operations, the *thin layer of tin which protects the mild steel sheet from rust* may be removed.

EXERCISE C *Relationships between statements*

Place the following words or phrases in the sentences indicated. Replace and re-order the words in the sentences where necessary. For examples, see Unit 1, Exercise C.

(a) because (1+2)   (e) however (13)   (h) because (17+18)
(b) namely (6)   (f) because (15+16)   (i) however (20)
(c) in addition (9)   (g) moreover (17)   (j) since (20+21)
(d) consequently (11)

EXERCISE D *Restatements using expressions of time*

Rewrite the following sentences, putting the expressions *before*, *while*, or *after* in the blank spaces so as to make statements which are correct according to the reading text.
1. Bending operations are performed on tin-plate . . . it has been cut to shape.

2. A mild steel ingot is rolled and pressed . . . it is white hot to produce hot-rolled sheet.
3. Bending allowances are calculated . . . the metal is marked out.
4. If tin-plate is scratched too deeply . . . it is being marked out, the layer of tin may be removed.
5. Hot-rolling of sheet steel takes place . . . it is cold-rolled to improve the finish.
6. Sheet metal is marked out . . . it is still in a flat form.
7. . . . mild steel has been cold-rolled it can be coated with a layer of tin.

EXERCISE E *Extracting information from the reading text*

Part 1
Classify by means of a diagram the three main types of sheet metal described in the text. (see Unit 4, Exercise D)

Part 2
Make a list of the different materials and operations which are mentioned in the text.

EXAMPLE

MATERIAL	OPERATION
sheet metal	bending
	marking out

EXERCISE F *Writing instructions for illustrations*

Study the following.

INSTRUCTIONS

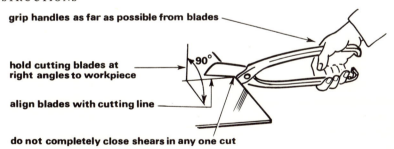

grip handles as far as possible from blades

hold cutting blades at right angles to workpiece

90°

align blades with cutting line

do not completely close shears in any one cut

ADVICE, OR RECOMMENDATIONS

You should grip the handles as far as possible from the blades. You should hold the cutting blades at right angles to the workpiece. You should align the blades with the cutting line. You should not completely close the shears in any one cut.

OR   The handles should be gripped as far as possible from the blades. The cutting blades should be held at right angles to the workpiece. The blades should be aligned with the cutting line. The shears should not be completely closed in any one cut.

INSTRUCTIONS can be changed into ADVICE or RECOMMENDATIONS in order to explain how something should be done, or to explain the best or safest way of doing something. In written instructions, note that the imperative form of the verb is used and that *articles* are *omitted*. When giving advice or recommendations, note that the auxiliary verb 'should' is used.

Part 1 Provide the illustrations on the following page with instructions using the information from recommendations given in paragraphs (a) to (f). Give a title to each illustration beginning *How to . . .* , e.g. (a) *How to use a file.*

(a) The correct size of handle should be fitted on the tang. The workpiece should be placed securely in the vice which should be positioned at the correct height. The workpiece should be placed as low as possible in the vice to avoid vibration and screeching. The correct stance should be adopted to maintain balance. The file should be kept square with the work and both hands should press down evenly on the file.

(b) A one-piece overall of the correct length should be worn. The buttons should be fastened and the sleeves tightly rolled up. Safety boots or shoes should be worn. No sharp tools should be carried in the pockets. Neither rings nor watches should be worn. Hair should be kept short, or protected.

(c) Chiselling should always be directed away from the body. The chisel should be held firmly at an angle of 30°–40° to the cutting plane. The elbow of the striking arm should be kept close to the body and the eye should be directed to the point of the chisel. Goggles should be worn and a chipping screen should be positioned in front of the work.

(d) The correct grade of blade should be chosen for the job. The work should be positioned close to the top of the vice. The cut should be started with the blade sloping at an angle of approximately 30° to the cutting plane. The handle of the hacksaw should be gripped firmly in one hand. The forward end of the frame should be held by the other hand.

(e) Goggles should be worn to protect the eyes. Protective clothing in the form of gauntlets and a leather apron should be worn. Gas and air lines should be in good condition and the connection between the torch and the gas and air lines should be checked. A screen should be placed in front of the work to protect other workers.

(f) The workpiece should be securely supported in a vice. A hole should be drilled to the tapping size of the thread. When starting the cutting, the tap should be at 90° in all planes to the work. The tap should be turned backwards after every forward turn to break up the swarf. Cutting fluid should be used.

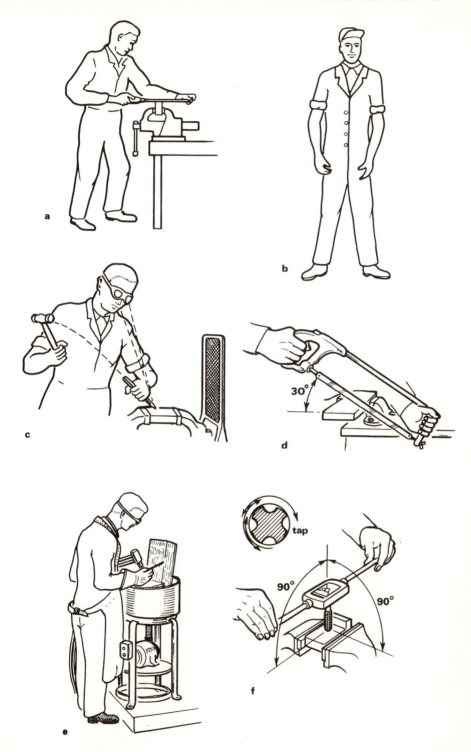

Part 2 Re-draw the diagrams for which you have written instructions in Part 1. Now LABEL them again as in the example below. Note that the past participle of the verb is often, but not always, included in the label.

EXAMPLE

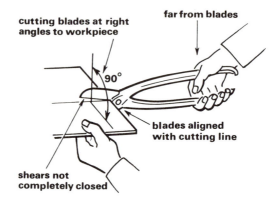

EXERCISE G *Writing recommendations and rules*

Part 1 Write short paragraphs which recommend how the following operations should be performed. Base your recommendations on the labels to the pictures.

EXAMPLE

How to hollow soft metal

A sandbag should be placed on the work-bench. The sheet of soft metal . . . etc.

(a) *Hollowing soft metal*

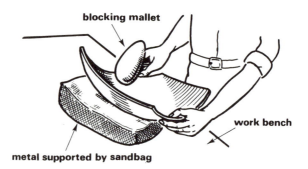

(b) *Upsetting a mild steel bar*

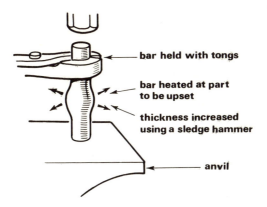

(c) *Cutting a metal bar with a chisel*

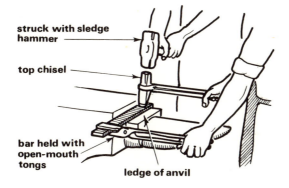

(d) *Thinning down sheet metal*

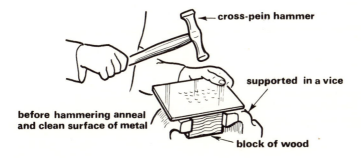

(e) *Keeping the work bench tidy*

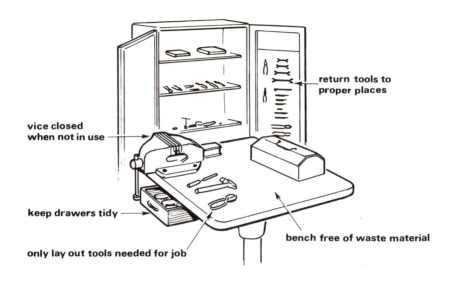

(f) *Drilling a hole*

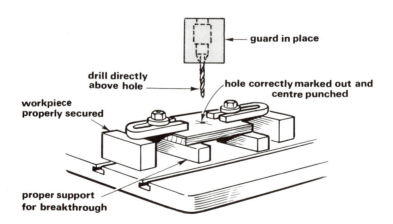

(g) *Annealing a work-hardened steel bar*

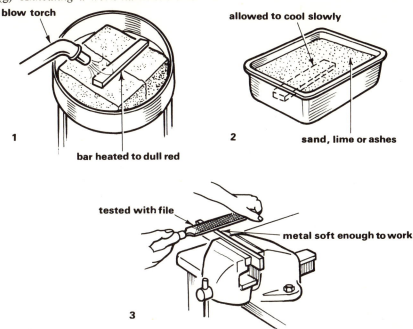

Part 2

Recommendations can be made stronger by using *must* instead of *should*.
Strong recommendations often become R U L E S, and therefore must be obeyed.

EXAMPLE

Rules for brazing

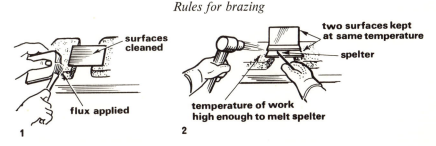

(i) The surfaces must be cleaned.
(ii) Flux must be applied.
(iii) The temperature of the work must be high enough to melt the spelter.
(iv) The two surfaces must be kept at the same temperature.
(v) The work must cool evenly to prevent cracking.

Look again at the recommendations in Exercise F, Part 1 and Exercise G,
Part 1 above. Where possible, change the recommendations to rules, using
must as in the example.

Part 3 We also have rules for safety in the workshop.

EXAMPLE

RULE: You must always use a file with a handle on the tang.

OR   A file must always be used with a handle on the tang.

OR   Never use a file without a handle on the tang.

OR   Always use a file with a handle on the tang.

OR   Don't use a file without a handle on the tang.

Write workshop rules to go with these safety posters.

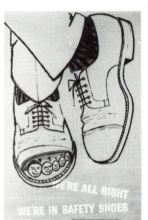

Reproduced by kind permission of ROSPA

II   GRAMMAR:
MODAL VERBS

(i) The pattern *it+to be+possible, necessary, impossible, unnecessary,* etc.

(ii) The modal verbs *can, cannot; may, may not; might, might not; must, must not; need, need not; ought to, ought not to; should, should not.*
   If a sentence contains the pattern given in (i) above, *it is nearly always possible to rewrite it* using a modal verb from (ii).

=   If a sentence contains the pattern given in (i) above, it *can nearly always be rewritten* using a modal verb from (ii).

The following sentences show the relationship between the meanings of (i) and (ii). Study them carefully before doing the exercise.

(a) *It is possible to* coat steel sheet with zinc.

Steel sheet *can* be coated with zinc.

(b) *It is possible that* sheet metal will crack if it is bent.

Sheet metal *may* crack if it is bent.

(c) *It is impossible to* cut metal with a hammer

Metal *cannot* be cut with a hammer.

(d) *It is possible that* the instructions are not very clear.

The instructions *may not* be very clear.

(e) *It is permitted to* make bends in the metal with a hammer.

Bends *may* (or *can*) be made in the metal with a hammer.

(f) *It is not permitted to* scribe metal with a chisel.

Metal *may not* (or *must not*) be scribed with a chisel.

(g) *It is essential to* inspect materials before they are used.

Materials *must* be inspected before they are used.

(h) *It is not essential to* temper a chisel every day.

A chisel *need not* be tempered every day.

(i) *It is advisable to* inspect safety guards regularly.

Safety guards *should be* (or *ought to be*) inspected regularly.

(j) *It is not necessary to* inspect every inch of the metal.

Every inch of the material *need not* be inspected.

(k) If the metal were not at the right temperature, *it is possible that* it would crack.

If the metal were not at the right temperature, it *might* crack.

(l) *It is forbidden* (or *prohibited*) *to* use this machine without the safety guard.

This machine *must* (or *may*) *not* be used without the safety guard.

(m) *It is inadvisable to* use a chisel on this material.

A chisel *should not be* (or *ought not to be*) used on this material.

(n) *It is compulsory to* wear gloves for this operation.

Gloves *must* be worn for this operation.

EXERCISE

Rewrite the following sentences using one of the verbs given in brackets instead of the expression in italics. Make any other changes in the sentence that are necessary.

1. *It is necessary that* the guard on a drilling machine is in place before the machine is switched on. (must, can, need)
2. *It is advisable that* welding equipment is carefully inspected for possible faults before it is used. (may, should, can)
3. When the wing nut at one end of a hacksaw frame is tightened, *it is certain that* the tension in the blade is increased. (will, may, should)

4. *It is permitted to* make angle bends in sheet metal by hammering the metal in a vice. (should, cannot, may)

5. Micrometers are precision-made instruments and *it is* therefore *necessary to* treat them very carefully. (can, should, need)

6. *It is recommended that* a hacksaw blade with 30 t.p.i. is used to cut sheet metal. (may, should, musn't)

7. While the end of a metal bar is being drawn down, keeping it at a bright red heat *is advisable.* (may, needn't, should)

8. *It is permissible to* use a surface grinder to produce a smooth surface on metal. (can, should, ought)

9. Where there is machinery with moving parts, *it is a rule that* sleeves are tightly rolled up above the elbows. (shouldn't, needn't, must)

10. After a mild steel bar has been forged or improperly heat treated, *it is possible to* restore it to its normal condition by the normalizing process. (can, must, will)

11. Using hand tools which are not properly earthed *is forbidden.* (needn't, shouldn't, musn't)

12. Wearing ties and scarves in the workshop *is prohibited* as they can get caught in moving machinery. (should, needn't, musn't)

13. *It is essential that* equipment used in electric arc welding is in good condition. (need, may, must)
    It is therefore *advisable to* inspect it regularly. (should, may, can)

14. Before welding with oxy-acetylene equipment *it is necessary to* adjust the flame correctly in order to obtain a good weld because too much oxygen *is likely* to contaminate the weld. (will, must, ought) (should, must, will)

15. Unless the correct forging temperature has been reached *it is definitely not possible to* forge the metal properly. (must not, will not, should not)

16. After annealing, a mild steel bar *is certain to* be malleable. (must, will, may)

17. *It is possible to* use hand-operated bench shears for the rough cutting of metal strips. (will, must, may)

18. *It is compulsory to* wear safety shoes in the machine tool workshop. (need not, may, must)

19. A well-ventilated forge is *essential* as the fumes given off from a coke fire are poisonous. (Begin: A forge . . .)
    (should, may, will)

8 Reading passages with comprehension questions

PASSAGE I

SOLDERING AND BRAZING

Soldering and brazing are metal joining processes in which a fusible alloy such as solder or spelter is bonded to the joint faces of the parent metals at a temperature below the melting point of those metals. The difference between these processes is in the temperature range over which they are
5 performed, and consequently the kind of heating process, and the type of filler metal used. Soft soldering is done at temperatures between 183°C and 327°C using solder as the filler metal. Silver soldering, or hard soldering, however, is performed at temperatures between 650°C and 800°C using a silver alloy. Brazing employs a fusible alloy called spelter
10 and takes place at a still higher temperature—between 850°C and 1000°C. Both soft and silver soldering can take place on the work bench. Brazing, however, is performed on a brazing hearth lined with special fire-bricks.

Soft soldering is done when the strength of the joint is not of primary importance. In view of the good conductivity of solder, it is used exten-
15 sively in electrical engineering, when connections between wires have to be made. Soft soldering is also useful in metal work when sheet metal joints have to be sealed so as to make them air or liquid tight. Silver soldering produces a harder joint than soft soldering and is used when copper, steel or brass components have to be soldered. When the joint
20 between steel or copper parts is required to be strong, brazing is the operation that is performed.

Soldering irons are used only in soft soldering and are of different sizes and shapes. There are two main types of appliance. Plain irons, which are heated on a gas ring, and electric irons, which have an internal
25 element to heat up the working head. Both types have copper bits attached to the head and both may be straight or hatchet shaped. For silver soldering and brazing a gas-air blow torch is used to obtain the higher

temperatures necessary. The gas is often acetylene, which, mixed with air
or oxygen, produces a very hot flame.

30   Before any kind of soldering can be done, the soldering iron must be
tinned. Tinning consists of cleaning the soldering iron while it is hot,
dipping it in a special flux and applying the solder. Fluxes are of two
kinds: those which protect the surface that has been cleaned, and those
which both protect the surface and help to clean it. The former, known as
35   passive fluxes, include rosin, tallow and gallipoli oil; the latter, known as
active fluxes, include zinc chloride and sal ammoniac, or ammonium
chloride. Different fluxes should be used for different jobs. Tallow for
example, may be used when joining lead pipes, while zinc chloride is used
for tin-plate and uncoated steel. For electrical work strips of solder can be
40   obtained which already contain the flux. Solder itself is an alloy of tin
and lead. The proportions of these metals may vary. Common solder may
have as much as 70% lead in it; plumber's solder, for soldering lead
pipes, may contain between 50% and 66·6% lead; tinman's solder, on
the other hand, has only 40% lead. Common solder contains a trace of
45   antimony. All solders, however, have a low melting point and are very soft.
For silver soldering and brazing the solder alloys are not a mixture of
lead and tin. Silver solder has silver in it in addition to copper and zinc.
Again, the proportions vary from 10% to over 70% silver according to
the type of metal to be soldered. Spelter for brazing is an alloy of copper
50   and zinc. For brazing cast iron, a spelter containing nickel may be used
which both strengthens the alloy and raises its melting point. The flux
for both these operations is usually borax. After silver soldering the work
should be dipped in dilute sulphuric acid to remove the flux. This is called
'pickling'. When silver soldering copper or brass parts, this operation can
55   be done before soldering in order to clean the parts.

EXERCISE A

Answer the following questions.
(a) How do metal joining processes differ according to temperature?
(b) Give two reasons why soft soldering is employed in electrical work?
(c) Which operation should be chosen when the strength of the joint is
    important?
(d) How is the head of an electric soldering iron heated?
(e) How is the high temperature of a brazing torch obtained?
(f) Why is a flux like zinc chloride known as an active flux?
(g) What property does solder have which makes it suitable for soldering
    work?
(h) How can spelter be made stronger?

EXERCISE B

Which expressions in the passage are used to describe the following:
(a) the original metal of the parts to be joined.
(b) the flat parts where the join is to be made.
(c) an alloy which has a low melting point.
(d) the metal which is used to fill the gap between the parts to be joined.
(e) the place where the brazing operation is performed.
(f) the part of the soldering iron which is used in the heating and fusing process.
(g) an instrument for heating that uses a mixture of gas and air or oxygen.

EXERCISE C

Copy out the following table and complete it using information from the passage.

	FUSIBLE ALLOY	FLUX	APPLIANCE	TEMPERATURE RANGE	USES
SOFT SOLDERING	....	rosin	soldering iron	....	....
	....	....	....		....
	....	....	....		....
	....	....			....
SILVER SOLDERING	silver solder	....	....	....	....
					....
BRAZING	....	....	....	850°C–1000°C	joining steel
					....
					....

PASSAGE II

WELDING

EXERCISE A

Read the following passage and write in your notebook appropriate expressions to fill the blank spaces, numbered (a) to (f). Your answer should be taken from the expressions given below.
(a) consequently, moreover, so, however.
(b) finally, briefly, generally, namely.
(c) on the other hand, as a result, nevertheless, in conclusion.
(d) thus, moreover, however, consequently.
(e) thus, however, on the other hand, briefly.
(f) moreover, however, on the other hand, consequently.

Originally, welding took place in the forge. The metal, usually wrought iron, was joined by hammering at a white heat. (a) . . ., true welding is the joining of the metals by fusion. A small area of the parent metals is melted together and allowed to solidify. (b) . . ., a filler metal of the same
5 composition as the parent metals is used. (c) . . ., a really strong joint is obtained.

Oxy-acetylene welding is a dangerous process and protective gauntlets and apron must be used and special goggles worn. Oxygen and acetylene when mixed in the correct proportion produce a flame as high as 3300°C
10 in its hottest part. Both gases are carried by a hose from cylinders to the blow pipe. Different sized nozzles are available which enable the welder to vary the heat of the flame and adjust its composition for reliable welds. Too much oxygen will cause brittleness in the weld whereas an excess of acetylene will result in carburizing. (d) . . ., an oxydizing flame is
15 necessary for welding brass and bronze, and a carburizing flame when welding stainless steel. Another type of welding is electric arc welding which produces an extremely hot spark of about 3300°C between the workpiece and an electrode. The electrode supplies the filler metal and is coated with a suitable flux for protection and cleaning.
20   The welding of wrought iron and mild steel by hammering is still done in the forge. It is performed by heating the shaped parts to the correct temperature and then hammering them together. The temperature required to do this is higher than that for ordinary forging. Wrought iron must be heated to a white heat (about 1350°C). At this temperature the
25 metal is soft and bright white sparks can be observed. Mild steel should be welded at a slightly lower temperature, a bright yellow heat. It is most important that the surfaces of the work are clean in order to obtain a good weld. (e) . . ., it is necessary to use a flux. Sand is suitable for wrought iron and borax is commonly used when welding mild steel. As the parts
30 are hammered together, a slag, formed from the liquid flux and impurities in the metal, must be forced out of the joint. (f) . . ., welding should begin at the centre of the joint and proceed outwards towards the edge of the work. This forces out the slag and leaves the welded surface clean. There are three types of joint used in hammer welding (see diagram below).
35 Butt welds are difficult to produce by hammering, but are common in oxy-acetylene welding. Scarf welds are the most common and the easiest to do. Vee welds are very strong. It is important that the faces of the parts to be joined should be properly shaped to facilitate the weld.

before
welding

after
welding

butt weld   scarf weld   vee weld

EXERCISE B

Answer the following questions:
(a) How is true welding to be distinguished from forge welding?
(b) Why is a welded joint strong?
(c) How does carburizing occur?
(d) Why is it desirable to be able to adjust the composition of the flame for particular welding jobs?
(e) How can two wrought iron parts be forge welded?
(f) What difference is there between the temperature necessary for hammer welding and for ordinary forging?
(g) At what temperature can white sparks be seen during heating operations?
(h) What is the purpose of using sand when welding wrought iron?
(i) Why is it necessary to remove the slag during welding operations?
(j) Why does hammering move outwards from the centre of the joint?

EXERCISE C

Define the following operations and substances by using expressions from passages I and II.

(a) soldering   (g) solder
(b) brazing   (h) spelter
(c) tinning   (i) fluxes
(d) pickling   (j) slag
(e) hammer welding   (k) a carburizing flame
(f) oxy-acetylene welding   (l) an oxydizing flame

PASSAGE III

MARKING OUT

EXERCISE A

Read the following passage and write in your notebook appropriate expressions to fill the blank spaces, numbered (a)–(f). Your answers should be taken from the expressions given below.
(a) moreover, alternatively, however, so.
(b) such as, for example, usually, however.
(c) so, moreover, finally, thus.
(d) consequently, on the other hand, conversely, however.
(e) moreover, nevertheless, so, also.
(f) moreover, nevertheless, however, so.

Marking out is the operation of drawing an outline of a component on metal before machining, drilling or filing operations are performed. There are three ways of marking out a workpiece. One way is to lay the work flat on a marking-out table and scribe the lines using a rule, engineer's
5 square and scriber. (a) . . ., the work may be placed perpendicular to the table top and marked with a surface gauge. A third method is to clamp the work to an angle plate with toolmaker's clamps. For the first two methods it is essential to have two datum edges to work from on the component. This can be done by filing two adjacent edges straight at 90°
10 to each other and to the face of the component. An engineer's square should be used to check these angles.

Before marking out, the surfaces are usually brushed with a suitable marking-out medium. (b) . . ., a solution of copper sulphate may be applied to bright mild steel. This is done after rubbing the surface with
15 emery cloth to brighten the metal. The copper sulphate is allowed to dry and a film of copper is (c) . . . deposited on the surface. The scribed lines will then have a silvery appearance and will be clearly visible.

It is important that scribed lines should be as fine as possible. This is to ensure the greatest degree of accuracy. (d) . . ., the fitter's tools should be
20 as sharp as possible. Dividers, calipers, scribers or the blade of a vernier height gauge should be checked for sharpness before commencing marking-out operations.

An outline that has been marked out with a scriber, and which is to be machined or drilled, should (e) . . . be witness dotted using a prick punch
25 or a spring-loaded centre punch. A larger hole can be witness dotted round its circumference. For smaller holes, (f) . . ., 'boxing' is preferable. 'Boxing' a hole assists in accurately positioning the drill during the drilling operations.

Most marking-out operations are done on a marking-out table because
30 rigidity and flatness of surface are essential for accurate work. The table is usually one of cast iron standing on four or more legs. The underside is usually ribbed. This prevents warping. The surface is made absolutely flat so as to provide a reference plane on which the work can stand together with the appropriate tools. When not being used, the working
35 face should be smeared with oil. The latter provides protection against rust, and, after it has been removed, leaves a smooth surface on which a surface gauge or vernier height gauge can move easily.

EXERCISE B

Answer the following questions.
(a) How can two datum edges be obtained?
(b) When can a surface gauge be used in marking-out operations?
(c) When is copper sulphate applied to the surface of a component?

(d) How does the use of a marking-out medium such as copper sulphate assist the marking-out operation?

(e) Why is it important that marking-out tools should be checked for sharpness?

(f) What operation should be performed after marking out if the outline is to be machined?

(g) How does 'boxing' help to ensure accurate drilling?

(h) Why is the flatness of the surface of a marking-out table essential for accurate work?

(i) How can the working face of a marking-out table be treated to prevent rust forming?

EXERCISE C

Make simple statements about the use of the following in marking out operations:

(a) surface gauge	(e) prick punch
(b) angle plate	(f) centre punch
(c) engineer's square	(g) copper sulphate
(d) emery cloth	

EXERCISE D

Describe what these diagrams show using information from the passage in addition to the labels in the diagrams.

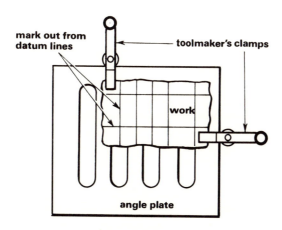

EXAMPLE

The work is clamped to an angle plate with tool maker's clamps. It is marked out from datum lines scribed on the work.

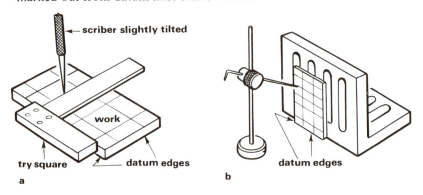

a   b

PASSAGE IV

THE DRILLING MACHINE

EXERCISE A

The blank spaces in the first paragraph of the following passage can be filled with expressions from Diagram 1. Similarly, Diagram 1 can be completed using expressions from the same paragraph. Rewrite the paragraph, inserting the correct expressions. Then draw the diagram and complete its labelling.

A sensitive drilling machine is a light high speed machine which is used for drilling small holes up to a $\frac{1}{2}$ in. in diameter. The machine consists of a column which is supported on a cast iron . . . which is bolted to the workbench. The drilling mechanism is mounted on a bracket which is
5 supported on top of the column. The drilling mechanism includes the motor and the drill head. On top is a belt drive and pulley system which is protected by a metal . . . . The motor and its . . . are located at the rear of the machine. On one side of the motor housing is the . . . . Positioned at the forward end are the spindle and the . . . protected
10 by a transparent guard. Mounted on another bracket on the column is a work table. It can be adjusted vertically between the . . . and the . . . and is secured by a . . . .

The drill is held perpendicular to the surface of the work. Rotary motion is provided by the electric motor and transmitted to the drill
15 spindle by the belt drive. The spindle speed can be changed by simply moving the belt to another set of pulleys. The drill is lowered, or fed, into the work manually so its progress can be felt. If any trouble occurs

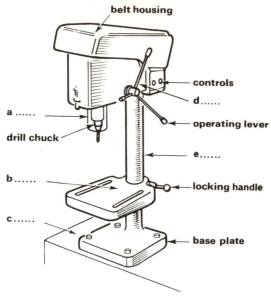

1 *A bench type sensitive drilling machine.*

the pressure can be released. On releasing the feed pressure, the spindle
returns to its uppermost position by means of a spring.

20   On a sensitive drilling machine, the drill is held in a chuck which has
three jaws. For use in a chuck, drills must have parallel shanks. They are
tightened with a special chuck key which has a peg on the end. This peg
is inserted into any one of three holes which are spaced at equal intervals
around the body of the chuck. By turning the key, the three jaws move

25 uniformly in or out. It is important that the drill is completely tightened
in the chuck. If it isn't, it will revolve in the jaws and this will damage the
drill. It should also be remembered that the shank of a drill is softer than

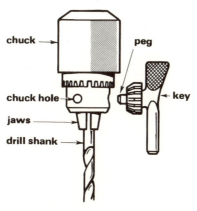

2 *A drill chuck*

the rest of the tool and can be bent. Therefore, it should not be used as a 'tommy bar' for such purposes as tightening a toolmaker's clamp. Once
30 the shank is bent, a drill is useless.

Before drilling the work should be gripped securely in a machine vice on the work table. Make sure that all the faces of the work are free from swarf or metal particles. The centre of the hole to be drilled should have already been marked out and centre punched. But some correction in the
35 position of the hole may be necessary before drilling if this is inaccurate. The position of the hole should be checked before the drill cuts a full diameter. If the hole is off-centre the error can be corrected by chipping a new centre for the drill in the work. This will allow the drill to be repositioned correctly. Once this has been done, the hole can be drilled in the
40 normal way.

EXERCISE B

Answer the following questions.
(a) How does the electric motor turn the drill spindle?
(b) Why is there more than one set of pulleys?
(c) How can the fitter feel the drill cutting through the metal?
(d) What happens when the fitter releases the operating lever while the drill is cutting through the metal?
(e) What type of drill must be used in a drill chuck?
(f) How are the jaws of the drill chuck tightened?
(g) What will happen if the drill is loose in the drill chuck?

EXERCISE C

What expressions in the passage and Diagram 1 are used to name the following:

(a) a machine which operates at high speed and does light drilling work
(b) the plate at the base of the drilling machine which is made of cast iron
(c) the belt which drives the drill
(d) the metal covering which protects the belt which drives the drill
(e) the handle which locks the work table in place
(f) the force which is needed to lower the drill into the work
(g) the metal component which holds the drill

FURTHER COMPREHENSION EXERCISES

INSTRUCTIONS, DESCRIPTIONS AND REPORTS

EXERCISE A

Study the following.

How to solder a ½″ lap joint of sheet metal

INSTRUCTION	DESCRIPTION	REPORT
(i) Clean metal surfaces to be joined.	*The* metal surfaces to be joined *are* clean*ed.*	The metal surfaces to be joined *were* cleaned.
(ii) Heat iron to correct temperature for solder being used.	*The* iron *is* heated to *the* correct temperature for *the* solder being used.	The iron *was* heated to the correct temperature for the solder being used.

A REPORT is a description of something done in the past. Continue writing descriptions and reports as in (i) and (ii) above, using the information given in the following instructions.

INSTRUCTION	DESCRIPTION	REPORT
1. Clean faces of iron with file or emery cloth.	....	....
2. Dip iron into flux and tin with solder.	....	....
3. Apply flux to metal surfaces to be joined and tin both surfaces.	....	....
4. Clamp two pieces of metal together.	....	....
5. Run clean hot iron over surface of joint so that solder is evenly distributed along joint	....	....

EXERCISE B

Change the following instructions into (a) a description and (b) a report, as practised above.

How to make a forge welded vee joint

1. Take two bars of black mild steel.
2. Heat one end of one bar to bright red, up to 35 mm.
3. Upset end on anvil face up to 35 mm.
4. Reheat upset end to bright red, up to 50 mm.
5. Grip bar in vice and split with hot set for about 35 mm down.
6. Upset one end of second bar to form slight bulge and form taper to suit the split.
7. Reheat first piece, open, and insert second piece into it.
8. Reheat ends of both pieces to bright yellow.
9. When correct temperature is reached, raise ends slightly above fire and throw on flux.
10. Replace in fire and raise to white heat.
11. Transfer to anvil, knock off scale. Hold each end with vee bit tongs and hammer from centre outwards.

EXERCISE C

Part 1 Change the descriptions in Exercise D, Part 1, Unit 6 and Exercise E, Part 1 and Part 2, Unit 6 into reports.

Part 2 Change the recommendations in Exercise F, Part 1, Unit 7 into reports.

Key to the Exercises

NOTE (1) In several exercises more than one version is possible. In such cases the key should be regarded as a guide only, and not as a complete or model answer.
(2) Exercises marked ① have been recorded. The recording is available on a single C 90 cassette published by Oxford University Press.

UNIT 1 – EXERCISES

EXERCISE A *Contextual reference*

1 (b), 2 b), 3 (a), 4 (c), 5 (c), 6 (a)

EXERCISE B *Rephrasing*

NOTE reference to where the replacing expression appears in the passage is given in parantheses.
1. *The dimensions* (1) of a small metal object can be measured by using calipers.
2. The legs of inside calipers curve *outwards* (11) at the points.
3. Some calipers have a spring which joins the legs together, but others *are stiff-jointed.* (16)
4. Spring calipers are *adjusted* (20) more easily than stiff-jointed calipers.

EXERCISE C *Relationships between statements*

(a) FOR THIS REASON, they are known as inside calipers.
(b) The legs of outside calipers are curved and turn inwards at the points, BUT those of inside calipers are straight and turn outwards at the points.
(c) AS A RESULT, the legs are kept open by means of friction.
(d) HOWEVER, not all calipers are of this stiff-jointed kind.
or: Not all calipers, HOWEVER, are of this stiff-jointed kind.
(e) FOR EXAMPLE, some calipers have a spring which joins the legs together.
or: Some calipers, FOR EXAMPLE, have a spring which joins the legs together.
(f) THEREFORE, they are known as spring calipers.
or: They are known, THEREFORE, as spring calipers.
(g) CONSEQUENTLY, calipers of this kind are more easily adjusted than the stiff-jointed kind.

EXERCISE D *Labelling of diagrams*

1. (a) legs
   (b) points
   (c) outside calipers

2. (d) stiff joint
   (e) inside calipers

3. (f) spring
   (g) nut
   (h) screw
   (i) spring calipers

EXERCISE E *The definition of objects in terms of class and use*

①**Part 1**

(a) A micrometer is an instrument which is used to measure small distances with precision.

(b) A pair of dividers is a tool which is used to scribe circles and radii.

(c) An engineer's square is an instrument which is used to check a right angle.

(d) Vee blocks are tools which are used to support round bars during marking out or drilling.

(e) A spirit level is an instrument which is used to set surfaces level.

(f) A scribing block, or surface gauge, is a tool which is used to scribe parallel lines on the work.

①**Part 2**

(a) Odd-leg calipers are instruments which are used to scribe lines which are parallel to an edge.

(b) A depth gauge is an instrument which is used to measure depths.

(c) Parallel strips are tools which are used to support work on the marking-out table.

(d) A vernier protractor is an instrument which is used to measure angles.

(e) A scriber is a tool which is used to mark lines on metal.

(f) An angle plate is an instrument which is used to support a surface at right angles to the marking-out table.

Part 3

Definitions from Part 1

(a) . . . which is used for measuring . . .
    . . . which measures . . .

(b) . . . which is used for scribing . . .
    . . . which scribes . . .

(c) . . . which is used for checking . . .
    . . . which checks . . .

(d) . . . which are used for supporting . . .
    . . . which support . . .

(e) . . . which is used for setting . . .
    . . . which sets . . .

(f) . . . which is used for scribing . . .
    . . . which scribes . . .

Definitions from Part 2

(a) . . . which are used for scribing . . .
    . . . which scribe . . .

(b) . . . which is used for measuring . . .
    . . . which measures . . .

(c) . . . which are used for supporting . . .
    . . . which support . . .

(d) . . . which is used for measuring . . .
    . . . which measures . . .

(e) . . . which is used for marking . . .
    . . . which marks . . .

(f) . . . which is used for supporting . . .
    . . . which supports . . .

EXERCISE F *General statements*

Part 1

(a) A micrometer is used to measure small distances with precision.

or: A micrometer is used for measuring small distances with precision.

etc. (compare the Key to Exercise E)

Part 2

(a) An engineer's rule is made of tool steel.

(b) The blade of a try-square is made of mild steel.

(c) A surface table is made of cast iron.

(d) Vee blocks are made of cast iron.

(e) The stock of a try-square is made of hardwood.

(f) Scribes are made of silver steel.

(g) A toolmaker's clamp is made of case-hardened steel.

(h) Centre punches are made of tool steel.
(i) Files are made of high carbon steel.

UNIT 1 – GRAMMAR

①EXERCISE A *Forms of definitions*
1. A die is a tool which is used for cutting an external thread.
A die may be defined as a tool which is used for cutting an external thread.
One may define a die as a tool which is used for cutting an external thread.
A (The) tool which is used for cutting an external thread is called a die.
A (The) tool which is used for cutting an external thread is known as a die.
2. Templates are patterns which are used for the fast marking out of difficult shapes.
etc. (as above)
3. A lathe is a machine which is used to turn and cut metal.
etc.
4. Plug gauges are instruments which are used for checking hole diameters.
etc.
5. Soldering is a process which joins metal to metal using a fusible alloy.
etc.
6. Silver steel is a ferrous metal which contains 98% iron, 1% carbon and 0·5% chromium.
etc.
7. Conductivity is the property which enables a metal to conduct heat or electricity easily.
etc.
8. A machine tool is a power-driven machine which is designed to hold a work-piece and cutting tool and produce a finished surface.
etc.

①EXERCISE B *The use of nouns and adjectives in definitions (shapes)*

(a) A tin can is a container in the shape of a cylinder.
A tin can is a container of cylindrical shape.
A tin can is a cylindrical container.
(b) Parallel strips are blocks of metal in the shape of rectangles.
Parallel strips are blocks of metal of rectangular shape.
Parallel strips are rectangular blocks of metal.
(c) A funnel is an instrument in the shape of a cone.
A funnel is an instrument of conical shape.
A funnel is a conical instrument.
(d) Ball bearings are objects in the shape of spheres.
Ball bearings are objects of spherical shape.
Ball bearings are spherical objects.
(e) A setsquare is an instrument in the shape of a triangle.
A setsquare is an instrument of triangular shape.
A setsquare is a triangular instrument.
(f) A straight edge is a strip of steel in the shape of a rectangle.
A straight edge is a strip of steel of rectangular shape.
A straight edge is a rectangular strip of steel.

①EXERCISE C *The use of nouns and adjectives in general statements (dimensions)*

1. (a) The metal plate is 50 mm wide.
The width of the metal plate is 50 mm.
The metal plate has a width of 50 mm.
The metal plate is 50 mm in width.

  (b) The component is 40 mm high.
     The height of the component is 40 mm.
     The component has a height of 40 mm.
     The component is 40 mm in height.
  (c) The hole is 10 mm deep.
     The depth of the hole is 10 mm.
     The hole has a depth of 10 mm.
     The hole is 10 mm in depth.
  (d) The steel strip is 250 mm long.
     The length of the steel strip is 250 mm.
     The steel strip has a length of 250 mm.
     The steel strip is 250 mm in length.
  (e) The steel tube is 10 mm in diameter.
     The diameter of the steel tube is 10 mm.
     The steel tube has a diameter of 10 mm.
  (f) The circular bar is 0·5 mm in radius.
     The radius of the circular bar is 0·5 mm.
     The circular bar has a radius of 0·5 mm.
  (g) The round bar is 50 mm in circumference.
     The circumference of the round bar is 50 mm.
     The round bar has a circumference of 50 mm.
2. (a) A steel strip, 30 mm by 5 mm by 60 mm long.
  (b) A metal tube, of 10 mm diam., 60 mm long.
  (c) A block of mild steel, 30 mm by 20 mm by 50 mm long.
  (d) A steel bar, 8 mm square, 15 mm long.
  (e) A metal plate, 2·5 mm thick.
  (f) A metal bar, of 15 mm diam., 25 mm long.

UNIT 2 EXERCISES

EXERCISE A *Contextual reference*

1 (b),   2 (b),   3 (b),   4 (c)

EXERCISE B *Rephrasing*

1. A micrometer can measure *with a precision of* 0·01 mm. (2)
2. There is a small anvil inside one end of the *semi-circular frame*. (4)
3. A spindle screws through the *barrel, or sleeve*. (7, 9)
4. The spindle is locked in position by a *locking ring*. (12)
5. If the spindle of a micrometer is *rotated* one *revolution* (19), the distance that it will move forward is equal to the pitch of the *screw thread* of the barrel. (18)

EXERCISE C *Labelling of diagrams*

(a) anvil   (b) semi-circular steel frame   (c) spindle   (d) barrel
(e) lock nut, or locking ring   (f) thimble   (g) ratchet

EXERCISE D *Description of a micrometer*

semi-circular, frame, anvil, frame, cylindrical, barrel, spindle, thimble, ratchet, lock nut, taken, spindle and the anvil, read off.

EXERCISE E *Description of objects*

Part 1

(a) A is attached to the top of B.
or: A is attached to B at the top.

(b) A is attached to the base of B.
or: A is attached to B at the base.
(c) A is attached to the left side of B at the top.
(d) A is attached to one end of B.
or: A is attached to B at one end.
(e) A is attached to the bottom of B.
or: A is attached to B at the bottom.
(f) A is attached to the base of B at right angles.
or: A is attached to B at the base at right angles.
(g) A is attached to the right side of B near the base.
or: A is attached to B on the right side near the base.

Part 2

(a) The wing nut of a hacksaw is attached to the forward end of the frame.
(b) The ratchet of a micrometer is attached to one end of the thimble.
(c) The legs of calipers are riveted to each other at the top.
(d) The blade of an engineer's square is set into one end of the stock at right angles to the frame.
(e) The clamps of a hacksaw are connected to the bottom of the handle and the end of the frame.
(f) The legs of dividers are connected to each other at the top with a spring.
(g) The handle of a file fits on to the pointed end of the body, known as the tang.
(h) The shaft of a hammer fits on to the head at right angles.
(i) The scriber of a scribing block is fixed to the side of the vertical spindle.
(j) The adjusting screw of a surface gauge is attached to one end of the rocker arm.

Part 3

(a) One end of A is circular.
(b) The top of A is rectangular.
(c) One end of A is round.
(d) The end of A is curved.
(e) One side of A is flat.
(f) The bottom of A is conical.
     The base of A is conical.
(g) One side of A is curved.
(h) The base of A is square.
(i) The surface of A is flat.
(j) The ends of A are pointed.

EXERCISE F *Re-ordering of sentences to build descriptive paragraphs*

1. A try-square consists of a blade and a stock. *The* blade is set into *the* stock at right angles. A brass strip may protect the face of the stock. It is held by steel pins.
2. Engineer's dividers consist of two flat strips of metal which are known as legs. *They* have pointed ends. *They* are connected part way down by a screw. A nut on *the* screw adjusts the setting. There is a spring at the top of the legs which keeps *them* open.
3. A ball-pein hammer consists of a head and a shaft. One side of the head is flat and called the striking face. The other side is curved and known as the pein. *The* shaft fits onto the head at right angles. *It* is secured with wedges.

4. A hand file consists of a rectangular body. *It* is cut diagonally by grooves. One end is pointed. This is called the tang. *It* fits into the handle. The end of the handle is protected by a ferrule.

5. A hacksaw consists of a frame. *It* is curved at one end. Attached to the other end is a handle. Clamps are connected to the bottom of the handle and the end of the frame. *The* blade is put in the frame with the teeth pointing away from the handle. A wing nut which is attached to the forward end of the frame adjusts the tightness of the blade.

⊕EXERCISE G *Definitions plus descriptions of objects*

1. A try-square is an instrument which is used for checking a right angle. *It* consists of a blade and a stock. *The* blade is made of mild steel, and *the* stock is made of hardwood. A brass strip protects the face of the stock. *The* blade is set into the stock at right angles. *It* is held by steel pins.

2. Engineer's dividers are tools which are used for scribing circles and marking off lengths and arcs. *They* consist of two flat strips of metal known as legs. *They* are made of hardened steel. The two legs are connected part way down by a screw. A nut on the screw adjusts the setting of the legs. There is a spring at the top of the legs which keeps *them* open.

3. A hand file is a tool which is used for cutting metal. *It* consists of a rectangular body which is made of hardened steel. *It* is cut diagonally by grooves. The pointed end of the body is called the tang. *This* fits into the handle. One end of the handle is protected by a ferrule.

UNIT 2 GRAMMAR: THE PASSIVE

⊕EXERCISE A

1. When scribing an angle on to a workpiece, the angle *is* first *measured* and afterwards it *is transferred* to the workpiece using a bevel gauge.

2. Small dots *are* accurately *punched* along the scribed line so that, when machining *is carried* out, the dots show that the marking out *has been worked* to.

3. The work *is set up* on the marking-out table and horizontal lines *are drawn* through the centres using a surface gauge. The work *is* then *turned* at right angles and lines *are drawn* through the centres again, perpendicular to those already drawn.

4. A vernier height-gauge *is used* for accurate marking out. It *can* also *be used* for measuring the height of a surface above the marking-out table.

5. A scriber *should be ground* to a sharp point before marking out because lines *should be scribed* on the work as fine as possible.

6. When marking out on bright mild steel, the surfaces *should be wiped* to remove oil and grease and then *should be rubbed* with emery cloth to brighten the metal. A marking-out medium, such as a solution of copper sulphate, *should* then *be applied* and *allowed* to dry completely. The film of copper which *has been deposited* on the surface enables the scribed line *to be seen* more clearly.

7. The surface of the marking-out table *must be kept* in perfect condition and *should be protected* with a film of oil when it *is not being used*. Care *should be taken* when placing tools on it and tools *should* never *be dropped* on it.

8. When using a steel scriber on a straight edge, the scriber *is held* at an angle to the straight edge and *inclined* in the direction of movement.

UNIT 3 EXERCISES

EXERCISE A *Contextual reference*

1 (a),   2 (b),   3 (c),   4 (c),   5 (a),   6 (a),   7 (a)

EXERCISE B *Rephrasing*

1. A fitter works on a bench which has a vice *bolted on it*. (3)
2. *A drilling machine* (6) can usually be found in the fitting workshop.
3. A surface grinder is used for *finishing* (11) work.
4. An off-hand grinder may be used for sharpening tools as *extreme accuracy* (13) is not required.
5. *A basic* (15) operation in bench work is hacksawing.
6. When the wing nut on the hacksaw frame is *tightened* (19) there is an increase in the tension in the blade.
7. Files are made from high carbon steel and *are very brittle*. (27)
8. Files *can be classified* (25) according to length, shape, and type and grade of cut.
9. The file should be pressed down with both hands *on the forward stroke* (30) but *on the return stroke* (31) it should be slightly raised.

EXERCISE C *Relationships between statements*

(a) He has various hand tools to work with SUCH AS files and chisels.
(b) FOR EXAMPLE, a surface grinder may be used for producing a smooth surface by removing small amounts of metal.
or: A surface grinder, FOR EXAMPLE, may be used for producing a smooth surface by removing small amounts of metal.
(c) HOWEVER, in order to sharpen tools such as cold chisels and screwdrivers an off-hand grinder may be used.
or: In order to sharpen tools such as cold chisels and screwdrivers, HOWEVER, an off-hand grinder may be used.
(d) In order to sharpen tools, such as cold chisels and screwdrivers, an off-hand grinder may be used BECAUSE for this kind of work extreme accuracy is not required.
(e) Hacksaw blades MAY BE CLASSIFIED according to the number of teeth per inch.
(f) For general use, one with 18 t.p.i. is satisfactory BUT for cutting thin sheet metal a fine blade of 30 t.p.i. is better.
(g) HOWEVER, others, called flexible blades, are hardened only along the teeth.
or: Others, HOWEVER, called flexible blades, are hardened only along the teeth.
(h) WE MAY COMPARE the cutting action of a file WITH that of a saw.
(i) THEREFORE, the file should be pressed down with both hands on the forward stroke.
or: The file should, THEREFORE, be pressed down with both hands on the forward stroke.
(j) ON THE OTHER HAND, on the return stroke, it should be slightly raised.
or: On the return stroke, ON THE OTHER HAND, it should be slightly raised.

EXERCISE D *Definitions of operations*

Part 1

(a) Chiselling is an operation by which excess material is chipped away from a large surface.
(b) Hacksawing is an operation by which metal bars and strips are cut.
(c) Hand-drilling is an operation by which a hole is machined in a workpiece.
(d) Off-hand grinding is an operation by which hand tools are sharpened.
(e) Reaming is an operation by which a hole is enlarged and finished to size.
(f) Scribing is an operation by which cutting dimensions are marked out.
(g) Riveting is an operation by which metal is joined to metal mechanically.

Part 3

	INSTRUMENT TOOL *or* MACHINE	VERB	PROCESS *or* OPERATION
(a)	file	to file	filing
(b)	chisel	*to chisel*	*chiselling*
(c)	*scraper* .	*to scrape*	scraping
(d)	*drill*	to drill	*drilling*
(e)	hacksaw	*to hacksaw*	*hacksawing*
(f)	reamer	*to ream*	*reaming*
(g)	*grinder*	*to grind*	grinding
(h)	*scriber*	to scribe	*scribing*
(i)	rivet	*to rivet*	*riveting*
(j)	*tap*	to tap	*tapping*
(k)	*screw*	*to screw*	screwing
(l)	bender	*to bend*	*bending*
(m)	lathe	to turn	*turning*
(n)	soldering iron	to solder	*soldering*
(o)	cold chisel	to chip	*chipping*

EXERCISE E *Generalizations*

Part 1
1.(a)

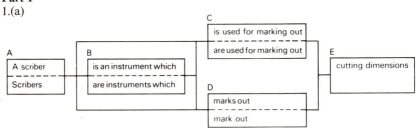

Definitions:
   A scriber is an instrument which is used for marking out cutting dimensions.
   Scribers are instruments which are used for marking out cutting dimensions.

Generalizations:
   A scriber is used for marking out cutting dimensions.
   Scribers are used for marking out cutting dimensions.
   A scriber marks out cutting dimensions
   Scribers mark out cutting dimensions.

(b)

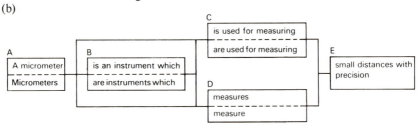

Definitions:
A micrometer is an instrument which is used for measuring small distances with precision.
Micrometers are instruments which are used for measuring small distances with precision.

Generalizations:
A micrometer is used for measuring small distances with precision.
Micrometers are used for measuring small distances with precision.
A micrometer measures small distances with precision.
Micrometers measure small distances with precision.

2. (a) a scraper, (b) a chisel, (c) a reamer, (d) a rivet
See Exercise D, Part 1, EXAMPLE, (a), (e), (g) and lay out as in 1 above.

Part 2

(a) We can check a right angle by using an engineer's square.
We can check a right angle with an engineer's square.
To check a right angle we can use an engineer's square.
We can use an engineer's square to check a right angle.
etc.

Part 3

(a) We can chip away excess material from a large surface by chiselling.
Excess material is chipped away from a large surface by chiselling.
Excess material can be chipped away from a large surface by chiselling.
(b) We can remove slight irregularities on a flat surface by scraping.
Slight irregularities on a flat surface are removed by scraping.
Slight irregularities on a flat surface can be removed by scraping.
(c) We can remove metal to produce a smooth surface by filing.
Metal is removed to produce a smooth surface by filing.
Metal can be removed to produce a smooth surface by filing.
(d) We can join metal to metal mechanically by riveting.
Metal is joined to metal mechanically by riveting.
Metal can be joined to metal mechanically by riveting.
(e) We can enlarge and finish a hole to size by reaming.
A hole is enlarged and finished to size by reaming.
A hole can be enlarged and finished to size by reaming.
(f) We can machine a hole in a workpiece by drilling.
A hole is machined in a workpiece by drilling.
A hole can be machined in a workpiece by drilling.

ⓘEXERCISE F *Writing descriptions from information in a table*

(a) A round file is used for opening out holes and rounding corners. It is circular (or round) in cross-sectional shape, with tapered sides. Smooth grades are single cut and rough grades are double cut.
(b) A square file is used for filing square corners. It is square in cross-sectional shape with tapered sides. All faces are double cut.
(c) A flat file is used for general surfacing work. It is rectangular in cross-sectional shape, with tapered sides. Both faces are double cut, and both sides are single cut.
(d) A half round file is used for filing concave surfaces. It is semi-circular in cross-sectional shape, with tapered sides. The flat face is double cut and the curved face is single cut.
(e) A triangular file is used for filing corners of 60° to 90°. It is triangular in cross-sectional shape, with tapered sides. All faces are double cut.

(f) A knife file is used for filing corners of less than 60°. It is triangular in cross-sectional shape, with tapered sides. The side faces are double cut and the narrow edge is single cut.

(g) A rasp file is used for filing soft metal. It is rectangular in cross-sectional shape with parallel sides. Both faces are rasp cut.

UNIT 3 GRAMMAR

①EXERCISE A *The use of* to+infinitive *in the expression of purpose*

1. (a) We set the teeth of the hacksaw at angles *to make* a cut which is wider than the blade.
   (b) The teeth of the hacksaw *are set* at angles *to make* a cut which is wider than the blade.
2. (a) We place the workpiece in the vice as low as possible *to avoid* vibration and screeching.
   (b) The workpiece *is placed* as low as possible in the vice *to avoid* vibration and screeching.
3. (a) We tighten the wing nut at one end of the frame *to increase* the tension in the bade.
   (b) The wing nut at one end of the frame *is tightened to increase* the tension in the blade.
4. (a) We anneal steel *to make* it as soft as possible.
   (b) Steel *is annealed to make* it as soft as possible.
5. (a) We can use the method of draw-filing *to produce* a good finish on a narrow surface.
   (b) The method of draw-filing *is used to produce* a good finish on a narrow surface.

① EXERCISE B *The use of* in order to+infinitive *and* so as to+infinitive

1. (a) Gloves should be worn when filing in order to protect our hands.
   (b) Gloves should be worn when filing so as to protect our hands.
2. (a) The file should be raised on its return stroke in order to prevent the dulling of the cutting teeth.
   (b) The file should be raised on its return stroke so as to prevent the dulling of the cutting teeth.
3. (a) Chalk should be rubbed into the teeth of the file during finishing work in order to prevent bits of metal clogging the teeth.
   (b) Chalk should be rubbed into the teeth of the file during finishing work so as to prevent bits of metal clogging the teeth.
4. (a) The hacksaw blade should be inserted with the teeth pointing away from the handle in order to cut material on the forward stroke.
   (b) The hacksaw blade should be inserted with the teeth pointing away from the handle so as to cut material on the forward stroke.
5. (a) The top of a marking-out table is machined flat in order to provide a good working surface.
   (b) The top of a marking-out table is machined flat so as to provide a good working surface.

①EXERCISE C *The statement of purpose in the first part of a sentence*

1. To check/in order to check the flatness of a surface, and its squareness to the face of the work, we should first use a try-square and a rule/a try-square and a rule should first be used.

2. To produce/in order to produce an internal thread by means of a tap, we must first drill a hole/a hole must be drilled of a diameter which is equal to the diameter at the bottom of the tap thread.

3. To avoid/in order to avoid damage to any finished surfaces on a workpiece by the hardened jaw pieces of the vice, we use false jaws of a softer metal, or even wood/false jaws of a softer metal, or even wood, are used.

4. To avoid/in order to avoid crooked hacksawing, make sure you have tightened the blade sufficiently/make sure the blade has been tightened sufficiently.

5. To avoid/in order to avoid breaking files and blunting the teeth we should put them/they should be put carefully in a tool box or on a rack.

6. To show/in order to show up a line very clearly, we brush the surfaces of the component/the surfaces of the component are brushed with a suitable marking-out medium.

7. To identify/in order to identify a particular file, we should know the shape, and type and grade of cut/the shape and type and grade of cut should be known.

8. To mark out/in order to mark out accurately, we must draw the lines/the lines must be drawn with a scriber as fine as possible.

9. To cut/in order to cut tubes or thin sheet metal, we should use a hacksaw blade/a hacksaw blade should be used with 30 t.p.i.

10. To mark/in order to mark the location of holes to be drilled, we use a centre punch/a centre punch is used in conjunction with a hammer.

①EXERCISE D *The use of* so that+clause *in the expression of result and purpose*

1. (a) We set the teeth of a hacksaw at angles so that we (can) make a cut which is wider than the blade.
   (b) The teeth of a hacksaw is set at angles so that a cut is (can be) made which is wider than the blade.

2. (a) We tighten the wing nut at one end of the frame so that we increase the tension in the blade.
   (b) The wing nut at one end of the frame is tightened so that the tension in the blade is increased.

3. (a) We use the method of draw-filing so that we (can) produce a good finish on a narrow surface.
   (b) The method of draw-filing is used so that a good finish is (can be) produced on a narrow surface.

4. (a) We hold the handle of a hammer at the end and not close to the head so that we can exercise greater control.
   (b) The handle of a hammer is held at the end and not close to the head so that greater control can be exercised.

5. (a) We anneal steel so that we make it as soft as possible.
   (b) Steel is annealed so that it is made as soft as possible.

6. (a) We should adopt the correct stance at the vice so that the filing arm can move freely.
   (b) The correct stance should be adopted at the vice so that the filing arm can be moved freely.

7. (a) A common fault when filing a flat surface is that we do not hold the file horizontally so that we produce a convex surface.
   (b) A common fault when filing a flat surface is that the file is not held horizontally so that a convex surface is produced.

8. (a) You should raise the file on its return stroke so that you prevent the dulling of the cutting teeth.
   (b) The file should be raised on its return stroke so that the dulling of the cutting teeth is prevented.

9. (a) We must keep the file teeth as sharp as possible so that they cut metal effectively.
   (b) The file teeth must be kept as sharp as possible so that metal is cut effectively.

UNIT 4 EXERCISES

EXERCISE A *Contextual reference*

1 (c), 2 (b), 3 (a), 4 (b) *or* (c), 5 (a), 6 (b)

EXERCISE B *Rephrasing*

1. The *basic material* (2) of ferrous metals is iron.
2. Non-ferrous *alloys* (5) include brass and bronze.
3. Cast iron is made from pig iron which has been *refined* (9).
4. Cast iron *is very brittle* (11).
5. Cast iron can be easily given a shape by *casting* (13).
6. Steel can be made by adding *known amounts of carbon* (17) to almost pure iron.
7. Plain carbon steels may be *classified according to* (21) their carbon content.

EXERCISE C *Relationship between statements*

(a) We may distinguish two groups of metals; those which contain iron, NAMELY, ferrous metals and those in which the basic material is a metal other than iron, NAMELY, non-ferrous metals.
(b) The former include cast iron, wrought iron, and steel, WHEREAS copper, tin, zinc and lead are examples of non-ferrous metals.
(c) FOR EXAMPLE, non-ferrous alloys include brass, which is made from copper and zinc, and bronze, which is made from copper and tin.
or: Non-ferrous alloys, FOR EXAMPLE, include brass, which is made from copper and zinc, and bronze, which is made from copper and tin.
(d) IN OTHER WORDS, cast iron is refined pig iron.
or: Cast iron is, IN OTHER WORDS, refined pig iron.
or: Cast iron is refined pig iron, IN OTHER WORDS.
(e) Cast iron is very brittle SO it will not bend.
(f) As cast iron is very brittle, it will not bend NOR can it be forged.
(g) HOWEVER, it is easily shaped by casting and some types can be easily machined.
or: It is easily shaped by casting, HOWEVER, and some types can be easily machined.
(h) Cast iron is THEREFORE used for making surface plates, vee blocks and marking-out tables.
or: THEREFORE, cast iron is used for making surface plates, vee blocks and marking-out tables.
(i) ALTERNATIVELY, it can be made by adding known amounts of carbon to almost pure iron.
(j) HOWEVER, if other elements are added, alloy steels are produced.
or: If other elements are added, HOWEVER, alloy steels are produced.
(k) FOR EXAMPLE, stainless steel contains both nickel and chromium, and the main element added to make most types of high speed steel is tungsten.
or: Stainless steel, FOR EXAMPLE, contains both nickel and chromium . . . .
(l) CONSEQUENTLY, it is used for making files, centre punches and hacksaw blades.
(m) It is used for making files, centre punches and hacksaw blades AND FOR THIS REASON it is known as tool steel.

EXERCISE D *Classification and levels of generalization*

Part 1

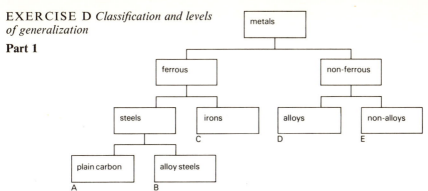

Part 2

A: mild steel, medium carbon steel, tool steel, silver steel.
B: high speed steel, stainless steel.
C: cast iron, wrought iron
D: bronze, brass.
E: copper, aluminium, zinc, lead, tin.

Part 3

(a) As in example.
(b) Copper is a non-ferrous metal.
Copper belongs to a class of metals called non-ferrous metals.
Copper may be classed as a non-ferrous metal.
(c) High speed steel is an alloy steel.
High speed steel is a ferrous metal.
High speed steel belongs to a class of metals called ferrous metals.
High speed steel may be classed as an alloy steel.
(d) Cast iron is a ferrous metal.
etc.
(e) Aluminium is a non-ferrous metal.
etc.
(f) Wrought iron is a ferrous metal.
etc.
(g) Zinc is a non-ferrous metal.
etc.
(h) Bronze is a non-ferrous alloy.
etc.
(i) Stainless steel is an alloy steel.
etc.
(j) Lead is a non-ferrous metal.
etc.
(k) Medium carbon steel is a plain carbon steel.
etc.
(l) Tool steel is a plain carbon steel.
etc.
(m) Brass is a non-ferrous alloy.
etc.
(n) Tin is a non-ferrous metal.
etc.
(o) Silver steel is a plain carbon steel.
etc.

Part 4

(a)

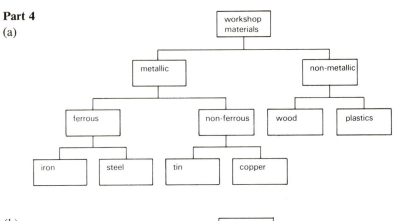

(b)

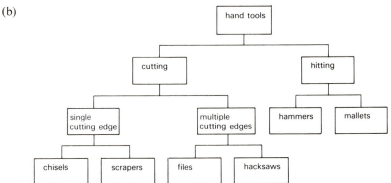

(c)

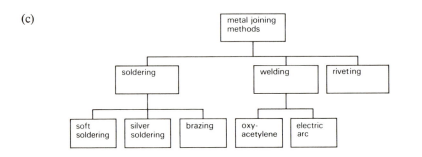

(d)

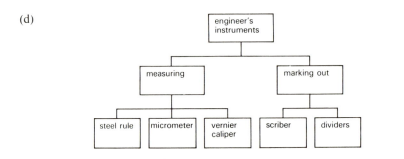

(e)

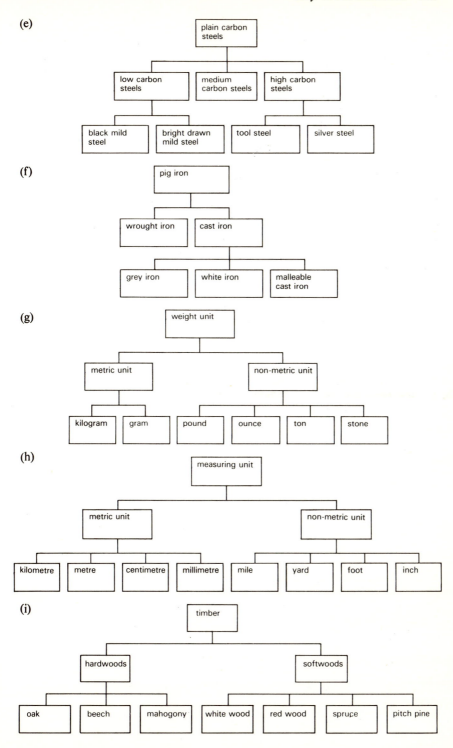

(f)

(g)

(h)

(i)

Part 5

1. Metals can be classified as *ferrous* and *non-ferrous*. The former may be divided into steels and irons, while non-ferrous metals may be divided into *alloys*, such as *bronze* and *brass*, and non-alloys, or pure metals, such as *aluminium, copper* and *tin*. Two kinds of steel may be distinguished: *Plain carbon steels* and *alloy* steels. Examples of the former include *tool* steel and *silver* steel. *Stainless* steel and *high speed* steel are examples of alloy steels.

2.(a) *Workshop materials:* as in examples.

(b) *Hand tools:* Hand tools can be divided into two kinds: cutting tools (or tools for cutting) and hitting tools (or tools for hitting). Two types of cutting tool can be distinguished: those with a single cutting edge, such as chisels or scrapers, and those with multiple cutting edges, such as files and hacksaws. Hammers and mallets are examples of hitting tools.

(c) *Metal joining methods:* Metal joining methods may be divided into soldering, welding and riveting. Three types of soldering may be distinguished: soft soldering, silver soldering and brazing. Welding methods are of two kinds: oxy-acetylene welding and electric arc welding.

etc.

NOTE These are only examples of classification paragraphs. Others are possible using a different arrangement of patterns shown in the table, as well as other constructions, such as:

There are three types of soldering: soft soldering . . .

We may classify hand tools into two kinds: . . .

Part 6

1. (a) Hand tools are usually made from *high carbon steel.*
   (b) *Cutting tools* are used for removing metal and should be kept sharp.
   (c) The basic materials in *pig iron* are iron and carbon.
   (d) *Metallic materials* expand when they are heated.
   (e) *Engineer's instruments* should be kept free from rust and dust.
   (f) *Marking-out instruments* are made from tool steel.
   (g) *Metal joining methods* can be dangerous, and require a great deal of skill and practice.

2. (a) Hand tools are usually made from hardened tool steel.
      Hardened tool steel is a high carbon steel.
      Therefore, hand tools are made from high carbon steel.
   (b) Cutting tools are used for removing metal and should be kept sharp.
      Diamond-point chisels are cutting tools.
      Therefore, diamond-point chisels are used for removing metal and should be kept sharp.
   (c) The basic materials in pig iron are iron and carbon.
      Malleable cast iron is made from pig iron.
      Therefore, the basic materials of malleable cast iron are iron and carbon.
   (d) Metallic materials expand when they are heated.
      Copper is a metallic material.
      Therefore, copper expands when it is heated.
   (e) Engineer's instruments should be kept free from rust and dust.
      A scriber is an engineer's instrument.
      Therefore, a scriber should be kept free from rust and dust.
   (f) Marking-out instruments are made from tool steel.
      Odd-leg calipers are marking-out instruments.
      Therefore, odd-leg calipers are made from tool steel.

(g) Metal joining methods can be dangerous, and require a great deal of skill and practice.
Oxy-acetylene welding is a metal joining method.
Therefore, oxy-acetylene welding can be dangerous and requires a great deal of skill and practice.

EXERCISE E *Classification according to defining characteristics*

Part 1

(a) Hacksaw blades may be classified according to the number of teeth per inch. For example, fine blades have 20 to 30 t.p.i. but coarse blades have 14 to 18 t.p.i.
(b) Scrapers may be classified according to the shape of the blade. For example, flat scrapers have a flat blade, but half-round scrapers have a curved blade.
(c) Hammers may be classified according to shape. For example, ball-pein hammers have round peins and a flat striking face, but cross-pein hammers have chisel-shaped peins and a flat striking face.
(d) Chisels may be classified according to the type of cutting edge. For example, flat chisels have a flat cutting edge but diamond-point chisels have a sharply tapered point.
(e) Plain carbon steels may be classified according to carbon content. For example, mild steel has less than 0·25% carbon but tool steel has up to 1·3% carbon.
(f) Files may be classified according to the type of cut. For example, single-cut files have cuts in one direction only, but double-cut files have cuts in two directions forming a diamond pattern.

Part 2

(a) A square file is a file which has a square cross-sectional shape.
(b) A flat scraper is a scraper which has a flat blade.
(c) A half-round scraper is a scraper which has a curved blade.
(d) A ball-pein hammer is a hammer which has a round pein and a flat striking face.
(e) A flat chisel is a chisel which has a flat cutting edge.
(f) A diamond-point chisel is a chisel which has a sharply tapered point.
(g) Mild steel is steel which has less than 0·25% carbon.
(h) Tool steel is steel which has up to 1·3% carbon.
(i) A double-cut file is a file which has cuts in two directions forming a diamond pattern.
(j) A single-cut file is a file which has cuts in one direction only.

①Part 3

(a) Ferrous metals may be classified according to whether carbon is deliberately added or not. For example, in steel carbon is added to strengthen the material, whereas in cast iron excess carbon is an impurity and must be reduced.
(b) Metal joining methods may be classified according to whether heat is used or not. For example, in welding metals are joined together by fusion, whereas in riveting metals are joined together mechanically using rivets.
(c) Steels may be classified according to whether carbon is the only element added or whether other elements are added. For example, plain carbon steel is made by adding known amounts of carbon to almost pure iron, whereas alloy steels are made by adding elements such as tungsten and chromium in addition to carbon.
(d) Engineer's instruments may be classified according to whether they are used for measuring or whether they are used for marking out. For example, micrometers and vernier calipers are used for measuring the dimensions of components, whereas scribers and dividers are used for drawing lines on metal.
(e) Non-ferrous metals may be classified according to whether the metal is in a

pure state or whether it is alloyed to another non-ferrous metal. For example, copper is a pure non-ferrous metal whereas bronze is an alloy of copper and tin.

(f) Hand tools may be classified according to whether they have a single cutting edge or whether they have multiple cutting edges. For example, chisels have only one cutting edge whereas files have many cutting edges from diagonal grooves which cross each other.

II GRAMMAR

①EXERCISE A *Defining and non-defining relative clauses*

1. A metal which can be spread out by hammering without cracking is malleable. (defining)

2. Bending and pressing and hammering of a metal often leads to a condition which is known as work hardening. (defining)

3. Brass, which is made from copper and zinc, is a non-ferrous alloy. (non-defining)

4. A fitter works on a heavy, rigid bench, which has a vice bolted on it. (non-defining)

5. A surface grinder may be used for producing a finish on metal which has been cut on another machine. (defining)

6. The working head of a soldering iron is usually made of copper, which is a good conductor of heat. (non-defining)

7. Some hacksaw blades are made from steel which has been hardened throughout. (defining)

8. A micrometer is an instrument which is used for measuring small distances very precisely. (defining)

9. Oxygen and acetylene, when mixed together, can produce a flame which reaches a temperature of about 3300°C. (non-defining)

10. Low carbon steel, which is also known as mild steel, contains up to 0·25% carbon. (non-defining)

11. The teeth of a hacksaw blade are set at angles so that the saw makes a cut which is wider than the blade. (defining)

12. There are two types of soldering iron: plain irons, which have to be heated on a gas ring, and electric irons, which have an internal element for heating. (non-defining)

13. A plain steel which has a low carbon content can be recognized by a stream of long white sparks which are produced when it is ground on an emery wheel. (defining)

14. Lead is a light grey metal which darkens quite rapidly when it is exposed to the atmosphere, which gives it a more familiar dark colour. (defining, non-defining)

15. The properties of irons and steels depend on the amount of carbon which has been added to them. (defining)

16. The cables which carry electric current to the various machines and tools in a factory are called conductors. (defining)

17. A hacksaw consists of a frame, which may be adjustable, and a blade, which is tensioned by a wing nut at one end of the frame. (non-defining)

18. The legs of spring calipers are opened or closed by means of a screw which is controlled by an adjusting nut. (defining)

①EXERCISE B *Short-form relative clauses*

Part 1

1. The vice *holding* the work on the fitter's bench must be at the correct height.

2. Typical objects *made* from medium carbon steel include springs, hammers, shafts and axles.

3. Steel is essentially an iron-carbon alloy *containing* less than 1·7% carbon.
4. Wrought iron is made by remelting and refining pig iron in a small furnace *known* as a puddling furnace.
5. Nickel steels are of two types: low nickel steels, *with* 3–5% nickel, and high nickel steels, *with* 25–40% nickel.
6. The main part of a micrometer is a semi-circular frame *with* a barrel *attached* to one end through which a spindle screws.
7. Usually in welding, the two materials *to be joined* together are of the same composition.
8. A flexible steel tape, *with* each inch or centimetre marked in uniform divisions, rolls into a case.
9. A hammer consists of a head, *made* of cast steel *with* a hardened striking face, and a shaft, *made* from well-seasoned wood.
10. Bench stakes are used to support work and have many different shapes and sizes *depending* on the article *being made* and the process *being carried* out.
(All the relative clauses are defining except those in 5, 8 and 9.)

Part 2
2. Bending and pressing and hammering of a metal often leads to a condition known as work hardening.
3. Brass, made from copper and zinc, is a non-ferrous alloy.
4. A fitter works on a heavy, rigid bench, with a vice bolted on it.
5. A surface grinder may be used for producing a finish on metal cut on another machine.
8. A micrometer is an instrument used for measuring small distances very precisely.
9. Oxygen and acetylene, when mixed together, can produce a flame reaching a temperature of about 3300°C.
10. Low carbon steel, also known as mild steel, contains up to 0·25% carbon.
13. A plain steel which has a low carbon content can be recognized by a stream of long white sparks produced when it is ground on an emery wheel.
15. The properties of irons and steels depend on the amount of carbon added to them.
16. The cables carrying electric current to the various machines and tools in a factory are called conductors.
18. The legs of spring calipers are opened or closed by means of a screw controlled by an adjusting nut.

UNIT 5 EXERCISES

EXERCISE A *Contextual reference*
1 (b),   2 (b),   3 (c),   4 (c),   5 (b)

EXERCISE B *Rephrasing*
1. It is usually ferrous metals that are forged by *hand processes*.
2. The steel plates of a forging hearth may be *riveted together*.
3. Located behind the forging hearth is the *bosh*.
4. The surface on which hot metal is shaped is called *the working face*.
5. The *punch hole, or pritchel*, can be used for *supporting* round metal bars during forging.

EXERCISE C *Relationships between statements*
(a) It (forging) MAY BE DEFINED AS the process of heating metal and pressing or hammering it into shape.

(b) Both ferrous and non-ferrous metals may be forged, ALTHOUGH it is usually the former that are forged by hand processes.

or: ALTHOUGH both ferrous and non-ferrous metals may be forged, it is usually the former that are forged by hand processes.

(c) BECAUSE the tuyere gets very hot, it has to be cooled.

or: The tuyere has to be cooled BECAUSE it gets very hot.

(d) THEREFORE, it passes through a tank of water which is known as the bosh.

or: It THEREFORE passes through a tank of water which is known as the bosh.

(e) THUS, the temperature of the fire can be adjusted by varying the amount of air which enters the tuyere.

EXERCISE D *Restatements*

(a) The fire-place in the middle of the hearth is lined with fire-bricks.

(b) Above the fire-place is a flue in the shape of a hood and fitted with a chimney.

(c) Behind the hearth is a blower driven by electric power.

(d) It passes through a tank of water known as a bosh.

(e) The temperature of the fire can be adjusted by varying the amount of air entering through the tuyere.

(f) The anvil supports the work to be shaped on a surface made of hardened steel.

(g) The anvil has a long and pointed beak used for bending metal bars.

(h) Rough work, such as cutting through metal with a chisel, is done on a step, or ledge, located between the beak and the table.

(i) The square hole, called the hardie hole, is used for putting the square shanks of bottom tools, such as the hardie and the fuller, in position.

EXERCISE E *Labelling of diagrams*

(a) chimney
(b) hood
(c) bosh
(d) tuyere
(e) fire-bricks
(f) power-driven blower
(g) fire-place
(h) forging hearth

(i) working face
(j) step, or ledge
(k) punch hole, or pritchel
(l) beak
(m) hardie hole
(n) cast iron stand
(o) anvil

EXERCISE F *Inductions, deductions and predictions*

Part 1

(a) If you pull a copper rod through a die, it will lengthen into a wire without cracking. This shows that copper is ductile.

(b) If you rub the surface of a tool steel bar with a fine file, it will leave no mark on the bar. This shows that high carbon steel is hard.

(c) If you hit a $\frac{3}{8}''$ diam. cast iron bar with a 1 lb hammer, it will snap easily. This shows that cast iron is brittle.

(d) If you heat a bar of lead to melting point, it will melt readily at a low temperature. This shows that lead is a fusible metal.

(e) If you place an aluminium rod on a piece of heat-sensitive paper and place one end of the rod in a flame, the paper alongside the rod will turn green quickly. This shows that aluminium is a good thermal conductor.

(f) If you hacksaw one-third of the way through a mild steel bar, place it in a vice and strike it with a hammer, it will break only after several blows. This shows that mild steel is tough and can absorb a great deal of energy before it fractures.

(g) If you put a bronze plate on two parallel steel bars and place a heavy load on the plate between the bars, the bronze plate will bend slightly, but if you then remove the load, the plate will return to its original shape. This shows that bronze is elastic.

Part 2

(a) If (*when*) a copper rod *is pulled* through a die, it will lengthen (it *lengthens*) into a wire without cracking.

(b) If (*when*) the surface of a tool steel bar *is rubbed* with a fine file, it will leave (it *leaves*) no mark on the bar.

(c) If (*when*) a ⅜″ diam. cast iron bar *is hit* with a 1 lb hammer, it will snap (it *snaps*) easily.

(d) If (*when*) a bar of lead *is heated* to melting point, it will melt (it *melts*) readily at a low temperature.

(e) If (*when*) an aluminium rod *is placed* on a piece of heat-sensitive paper and one end of the rod *is placed* in a flame, the paper alongside the rod will turn (*turns*) green quickly.

(f) If (*when*) a mild steel bar *is hacksawed* one-third of the way through, *placed* in a vice and *struck* with a hammer, it will break (it *breaks*) only after several blows.

(g) If (*when*) a bronze plate *is put* on two parallel steel bars, a heavy load placed on the plate and afterwards *removed*, the bronze plate will return (*returns*) to its original shape.

Part 3

(a) If you pull a copper rod through a die it will lengthen into a wire without cracking.

This shows that
Thus,
Hence,
Therefore, } copper is ductile.
This demonstrates that,
This indicates that,

(b)–(g) See Part 1, above.

Part 4

(a) Copper is ductile. Thus (therefore, hence, consequently) if you pull a copper rod through a die, it will lengthen into a wire without cracking.

(b)–(g) See Part 1, above.

Part 5

(a) Copper is ductile. For example, if you pull a copper rod through a die, it will lengthen into a wire without cracking.

(b)–(g) See Part 1, above.

NOTE The expression *for example* may appear in different places in the structure. e.g. Copper is ductile. If, for example, you pull a copper rod. . . .

Part 6

Copper has the property of ductility.
Lead has the property of fusibility.
Aluminium has the property of good thermal conductivity.
Bronze has the property of elasticity.
High carbon steel has the property of hardness.
Cast iron has the property of brittleness.
Mild steel has the property of toughness.
NOTE The suffixes '-ness' and '-ity' express qualities or characteristics.

Part 7

(a) 1 (d)   5 (g)
    2 (f)   6 (h)
    3 (e)   7 (b)
    4 (c)   8 (a)

1. Malleability is the property which enables a metal *to be shaped* by hammering without cracking.
2. Ductility is the property which enables a metal *to be drawn out* into a wire without cracking.
3. Fusibility is the property which enables a metal *to melt* readily at a low temperature.
4. Conductivity is the property which enables a metal *to conduct* heat or electricity.
5. Elasticity is the property which enables a metal *to return* to its original shape after a heavy load has been removed.
6. Hardness is the property which enables a metal to *resist* scratching, wear and abrasion.
7. Toughness is the property which enables a metal *to absorb* a great deal of energy without fracturing.
8. Brittleness is the property which causes* a metal *to break* easily when hit with a hammer.

(b) 1. A metal which *can be shaped* by hammering without cracking possesses the property of malleability.
2. A metal which *can be bent or drawn out* into a wire without cracking possesses the property of ductility.
etc. See (a) above.

*Note that brittleness is an *undesirable* property. Therefore, the verb *cause* rather than *enable* is more appropriate.

Part 8

(a) Ductility is the property which enables a metal to be drawn out into a wire without cracking. Copper is ductile; therefore, if you pull a copper rod through a die, it lengthens into a wire without cracking.
etc. See Part 7+Part 1 above.

UNIT 5 GRAMMAR

①EXERCISE A *Relative clauses introduced by a preposition*

1. Forging is a process *in which* heated metal is shaped by hammering.
2. A vice consists of a cast iron or steel body *into which* is fitted a square section insert shaped into a jaw at its outer end.
3. The majority of metals *with which* an engineer has to deal are metallic.
4. The edges of a swage block have a series of grooves *on which* heavy work can be swaged.
5. Welding is a joining process *in which* a small area of the parent metal is melted and allowed to solidify.
6. Grey iron is the principal material *from which* iron castings are made.
7. Pig iron is the raw material *from which* cast irons and steels are made.
8. The temperature *at which* wrought iron may be successfully welded is about 1300°C.

①EXERCISE B *Noun+noun constructions*

  1. — is an alloy which contains aluminium.
  2. — is a swage with a spring.

3. — is a table with a (flat or smooth) surface.
4. — is steel which is used for cutting metal at a high speed.
5. — is a chisel with a point which is shaped like a diamond.
6. — is a belt which is used for conveying (or carrying) objects along.
7. — are tongs which are used for picking up hot metal.
8. — is forging which is done by hand.
9. — are tools which are used for marking out.
10. — are bristles which are made from wire.
11. — are gloves which are made from asbestos.
12. — are the buttons of an overall.
13. — is a vehicle which is operated by a motor.
14. — is the blade of a hacksaw.
15. — is the box (of a machine) which contains the gears.
16. — is a cylinder which contains gas.
17. — is bronze which contains manganese.
18. — are calipers with a vernier scale.
19. — is a plate with a flat surface.
20. — is a nut which is used for locking.
21. — is treatment (of metal) by heat, or which uses heat.
22. — are the threads of a screw.
23. — is the head of a hammer.
24. — is the bed of a machine.
25. — is a gauge which is used for measuring depth.
26. — are tools which are operated by machine.
27. — is a stand which is made from cast iron.
28. — is the diameter of a wheel.
29. — are blocks which are shaped like a vee (v).
30. — is a hole which is used for holding hardies.
31. — is an apron which is made from leather.
32. — are nuts which are shaped like wings.
33. — is a bar which is made from metal.
34. — is a tank which is used for quenching.
35. — is the joint of two pieces of metal.
36. — is a mould which is made from sand.
37. — are plates of metal which are made from steel.
38. — is a tank which is used for holding petrol.
39. — are pipes for water.
40. — is a motor which is used for driving (the drill).
41. — is a hacksaw which is operated by power.
42. — is a rule which is made from steel.
43. — are tools which are used for pressing.
44. — is soldering which uses silver.
45. — is bronze which contains phosphor.
46. — is steel which is like a sheet.
47. — are tools which are operated by (electric) power.
48. — is a wheel which is shaped like a star.
49. — are pipes for air.
50. — is solder which is in the shape of a bar.
51. — is a tool which is used for cutting pipes.
52. — is an instrument which is used for regulating gas.
53. — is an instrument which is used for holding tools.
54. — is the guard of a drill chuck.
55. — is someone who operates a lathe.

①EXERCISE C *Noun+participle constructions*

1. scribing   2. hardened   3. locking . . . tempering   4. ventilated
5. shaped   6. hardened . . . striking . . . seasoned   7. cutting . . . grinding
8. operated   9. driven   10. machining   11. fitting 12. moving
13. measuring

①EXERCISE D *Complex noun phrases*

1. power operated guillotines
2. hexagon shaped tool carrier
3. hand held power tools
4. electric arc welding
5. flux coated electrode
6. roller type bending machine
7. blast regulating valves
8. motor vehicle cylinder blocks
9. hardened cast steel working face
10. work hardened mild steel bar
11. compressed air cylinders . . . inflammable acetylene gas cylinders
12. high speed steel cutting tools

UNIT 6 EXERCISES

EXERCISE A *Contextual reference*

1 (a),   2 (b),   3 (c),   4 (c),   5 (a),   6 (b),

EXERCISE B *Rephrasing*

1. A chisel is *quenched* after it has been heated to a cherry red colour.
2. *Annealing restores* a metal to *its original condition.*
3. Annealing can be performed on a carbon steel bar which has become *work-hardened.*
4. It is important that steel which is being annealed should not be *overheated.*
5. *Brittleness* can be reduced by *tempering.*

EXERCISE C *Relationships between statements*

(a) HOWEVER, a metal which has become work-hardened in this way can be made softer and more workable again.
or: A metal which has become work-hardened in this way can, HOWEVER, be made softer and more workable again.
(b) THE NAME OF THE PROCESS FOR doing this is annealing.
or: Annealing is THE NAME OF THE PROCESS FOR doing this.
(c) HOWEVER, great care should be taken not to overheat the metal.
or: Great care should be taken, HOWEVER, not to overheat the metal.
(d) THEREFORE it has to be hardened.
or: It THEREFORE has to be hardened.
(e) After that, it is plunged vertically into cold water, and moved about rapidly IN ORDER TO prevent cracking.
(f) AS A RESULT the steel BECOMES very hard, but brittle.
(g) THEN the metal is heated and the different colours which appear on the metal noted.
or: The metal is THEN heated and the different colours which appear on the metal noted.
(h) IT WILL BE FOUND THAT the chisel is hard, but now less brittle.

EXERCISE D *Description of an operation and its result*

①**Part 1**   *List A*   *List B*

(a)	3	iv
(b)	1	vi
(c)	5	ii
(d)	6	i
(e)	2	v
(f)	4	iii

(a) The work-hardened steel bar is heated to dull red and allowed to cool slowly in sand or ashes. It is (then) tested with a file. It will be found that the metal's malleability is restored, which makes it workable again. (*or:* . . . making it workable again.)

(b) The mild steel component is heated to bright red. It is (then) dipped in a carbon rich mixture. The process is repeated to ensure sufficient carbon intake. It will be found that the component absorbs carbon into its surface layer, which makes it very hard when suitably heat treated. (*or:* Carbon is absorbed into the surface layer of the component, which makes it very hard when suitably heat treated.)

(c) The chisel is heated to cherry red. It is (then) plunged vertically into the cold water and moved about rapidly to prevent cracking. It will be found that this makes the chisel very hard but brittle. (*or:* The chisel is made very hard but brittle.)

(d) The component is heated to the same temperature as for hardening. It is (then) left to cool freely in draught-free air. It will be found that stresses set up in the metal during cold working are removed and the metal is returned to its normal condition.

(e) The bar is heated at the part to be upset. One end of the bar is (then) struck with a hammer. It will be found that this increases the thickness of the metal bar at the expense of its length. (*or:* The thickness of the metal bar is increased at the expense of its length.)

(f) The bar is heated at the point to be drawn down. The length of the bar is (then) increased by using a fuller. It is finished with a flatter. It will be found that this increases the length of the bar but decreases the width and thickness. (*or:* The length of the bar is increased but the width and thickness decreased.)

Part 3 (See Exercise F, Part 1, Unit 5)

(a) A copper rod is pulled through a die.
It will be found that the rod will lengthen into a wire without cracking,
or: It will be found that the rod can be lengthened into a wire without cracking.

(b) The surface of a tool steel bar is rubbed with a fine file.
It will be found that the file leaves no mark on the bar.
or: It will be found that no mark is left on the bar.

(c) A $\frac{3}{8}''$ diam. cast iron bar is hit with a 1 lb hammer.
It will be found that the bar snaps easily.
or: It will be found that the bar can be snapped easily.

(d) A bar of lead is heated to melting point.
It will be found that the bar melts readily at a low temperature.
or: It will be found that the bar can be melted readily at a low temperature.

(e) An aluminium rod is placed on a piece of heat-sensitive paper and one end of the rod is placed in a flame.
It will be found that the paper alongside the rod turns green quickly.

(f) A mild steel bar is hacksawed one-third of the way through, placed in a vice and struck with a hammer.
It will be found that the bar breaks only after several blows.
or: It will be found that the bar can be broken only after several blows.

(g) A bronze plate is put on two parallel steel bars, a heavy load is placed on the plate, and afterwards removed.
It will be found that the bronze plate bends slightly at first but afterwards returns to its original shape.

Part 4

1. (a) To anneal a work-hardened steel bar, the bar is *first* heated to dull red and *then* allowed to cool slowly in sand or ashes. It is tested with a file. This restores the metal's malleability, which makes it workable again.
(b) To carburize, or case harden, a mild steel component, it is *first* heated to bright red and *then* dipped in a carbon rich mixture. The process is repeated to ensure sufficient carbon intake. The component absorbs carbon into its surface layer, which makes it very hard after suitable heat treatment.
(c) To harden a chisel . . .
(d) To normalize a metal component . . .
(e) To upset a metal bar . . .
(f) To draw down a metal bar . . .
2. (a) To show/demonstrate that copper is ductile, a copper rod is pulled through a die. It will be found that it lengthens into a wire without cracking.
(b) To show/demonstrate that high carbon steel is hard . . .
(c) To show/demonstrate that cast iron is brittle . . .
(d) To show/demonstrate that lead is a fusible metal . . .
(e) To show/demonstrate that aluminium is a good thermal conductor, an aluminium rod is *first* placed on a piece of heat-sensitive paper and *then* one end of the rod is placed in a flame. It will be found that the paper alongside the rod turns green quickly.
(f) To show that mild steel is tough and can absorb a great deal of energy, a mild steel bar is *first* hacksawed one-third of the way through. *Then,* (next) it is placed in a vice and (then) struck with a hammer. It will be found that it breaks only after several blows.
(g) To show that bronze is elastic/has the property of elasticity/, a bronze plate is *first* put on two parallel steel bars. A heavy load is placed on the plate and *then* afterwards removed. The bronze plate bends slightly at first but afterwards it returns to its original shape.

①Part 5

(a) If a work-hardened steel bar is heated to dull red, allowed to cool slowly in sand or ashes and then tested with a file, the metal's malleability is restored. Thus, annealing makes a work-hardened steel bar workable again.
(b) If a mild steel component is heated to bright red and dipped in a carbon rich mixture, the component absorbs carbon into its surface layer. Thus, carburizing makes a component very hard after suitable heat treatment.
(c) If a chisel is heated to cherry red, plunged vertically into cold water and moved about rapidly to prevent cracking, the chisel is made very hard but brittle. The process is called hardening.
(d) If a component is heated to the same temperature as for hardening and left to cool freely in draught-free air, the stresses set up in the metal during cold working are removed. Thus, normalizing a metal component returns it to its normal un-stressed condition.
(e) If a bar is heated at the part to be upset and one end is struck with a hammer, the thickness of the bar is increased at the expense of its length. This process is called upsetting.
(f) If a bar is heated at the point to be drawn down and the length of the bar

increased by using a fuller, the length of the bar is increased but the width and thickness are decreased. This process is called drawing down.

EXERCISE E *Instructions based on descriptions*

Part 1

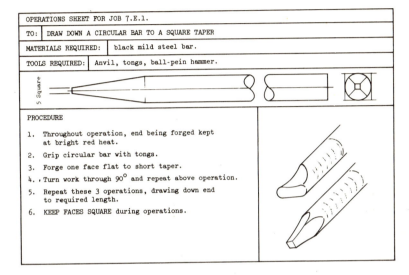

OPERATIONS SHEET FOR JOB 7.E.1.

TO: DRAW DOWN A CIRCULAR BAR TO A SQUARE TAPER

MATERIALS REQUIRED: black mild steel bar.

TOOLS REQUIRED: Anvil, tongs, ball-pein hammer.

5 Square

PROCEDURE

1. Throughout operation, end being forged kept at bright red heat.
2. Grip circular bar with tongs.
3. Forge one face flat to short taper.
4. Turn work through 90° and repeat above operation.
5. Repeat these 3 operations, drawing down end to required length.
6. KEEP FACES SQUARE during operations.

Part 2

1.

OPERATIONS SHEET FOR JOB 7.E.2.

TO: DRAW DOWN A SQUARE BAR TO A CIRCULAR TAPER

MATERIALS REQUIRED: black mild steel bar.

TOOLS REQUIRED: Anvil, vee-bit tongs, ball-pein hammer.

PROCEDURE:

1. Throughout operation, end being forged kept at bright red heat.

2. Forge one end to square taper, 75mm long.

3. Place work on anvil face so that corner of tapered portions is touching anvil and faces are 45° to top of anvil.

4. Forge opposite faces to octagonal pyramid shape.

5. Lightly hammer corners of bar to conical shape with 5mm dia nose.

2.

OPERATIONS SHEET FOR JOB 7.E.3.	
TO:	MANUFACTURE A COLD CHISEL
MATERIALS REQUIRED:	Octagonal bar, 0.8% high carbon steel.
TOOLS REQUIRED:	Anvil, ball-pein hammer, tongs, quenching bath, off-hand grinding machine.

PROCEDURE:

1. Throughout operation bar heated to bright red.
2. Hold bar at slight angle on anvil face.
3. Draw down one face to wedge shape.
4. Turn bar through 180° and draw down opposite face to wedge shape.
5. Reverse bar and forge champfer on striking end.
6. Allow bar to cool slowly.
7. Roughly grind cutting edge, then harden and temper.
8. Finish-grind cutting edge on grinding machine and test quality on a mild steel block.

II GRAMMAR

⓪EXERCISE A *Time expressions:* after, before, when, as soon as, while, until

Part 1

1. *When* a carbon steel bar has been struck repeatedly, it becomes work-hardened.
2. *As soon as* the temper colour reaches purple, the chisel is quenched in water.
3. *After* a mild steel bar has been annealed, it is tested for workability with a file.
4. *Before* the operations of hacksawing, drilling and filing are performed in the fitting workshop, the metal has to be marked out accurately on a marking-out table.
5. *While* the operation of drawing down is taking place, the end which is being forged is kept at a bright red heat.
6. *After* sheet metal has been marked out and cut to size, it has to be formed into its final shape.
7. *After* a mild steel bar has been annealed, it is restored to its original condition.
8. *When* a surface has to be scraped by a scraper with strokes in one direction, it must be scraped with strokes at 90° to the first ones.
9. *When* metal is hardened, it can become brittle.
10. *When* the wing nut at one end of a hacksaw is tightened, the tension of the blade is increased.

Part 2

1. A carbon steel bar does *not* become work-hardened *until* it has been struck repeatedly.
2. The chisel is *not* quenched in water *until* the temper colour reaches purple.
4. The operation of hacksawing, chiselling and filing are *not* performed in the fitting workshop *until* the metal has been marked out accurately on a marking-out table.
6. *Until* sheet metal has been marked out and cut to size, it *cannot* be formed into its first shape.
7. *Until* it has been annealed, a mild steel bar is *not* restored to its original condition.
8. A surface grinder can *not* be used to produce a smooth surface on a metal bar *until* it (the bar) has been roughly cut with a power hacksaw.

EXERCISE B *Time expressions:* then, during, throughout, prior to, first

1. X   2. √   3. X   4. √   5. √   6. X   7. √   8. X   9. √   10. √
11. X   12. √

ⓘEXERCISE C *Short-form time clauses*

1. After being heated to dull red, the metal is allowed to cool slowly in sand.
2. After being hacksawed ⅓ of the way through, the mild steel bar is placed in a vice and struck with a hammer until it breaks.
3. Before starting to cut a thread with a tap, we must drill the right size of hole depending on the root diameter of the thread.
4. While being drawn down, the end of the metal bar should be kept at a bright red heat.
5. After being kept at high temperatures, a mild steel bar can have its structure refined by normalizing.
6. When measuring the diameter of a round bar, calipers should just touch the bar as they are passed over it.
7. On being hammered to shape, a wrought iron bar spreads out without cracking.
8. Before being bent and pressed, sheet metal is marked out and cut to shape.

UNIT 7 EXERCISES

EXERCISE A *Contextual reference*

1 (a),   2 (b),   3 (b),   4 (a),

EXERCISE B *Rephrasing*

1. It is essential that the metal used in sheet metal work should have the property *of malleability*. (1)
2. *Hot-rolled sheet steel* (5) can be cold-rolled to produce a brighter better finish.
3. *Tin-plate* (7) can be marked out with a scriber.
4. *Galvanized sheet steel* (11) is protected from rust by the zinc coating.
5. *A sheet metal worker* (14) must have a knowledge of geometry.
6. It is essential that *bending allowances* (18) should be calculated and marked off.
7. If tin-plate is scratched too deeply with a scriber during marking-out operations the *protective coating* (21) may be removed.

EXERCISE C *Relationships between statements*

(a) Sheet metal must possess the property of malleability BECAUSE once the material has been cut to shape, bending and pressing operations are performed on it.
(b) A further process, NAMELY cold-rolling, produces a surface which is brighter and which has a better finish.
(c) IN ADDITION, iron or steel sheet can be coated with zinc on each side.
(d) CONSEQUENTLY, the material produced is known as galvanized sheet iron or steel.
(e) HOWEVER, zinc gives a better protective coating for steel than tin does.
or: Zinc, HOWEVER, gives a better protective coating for steel than tin does.
(f) A knowledge of geometry is required BECAUSE the three dimensional finished shape of an object never looks the same as its shape when it is marked out on flat metal.
(g) MOREOVER, it is essential to calculate and mark off enough metal to allow for bending and folding.
or: It is essential, MOREOVER, to calculate and mark off enough metal to allow for bending and folding.

(h) It is essential, moreover, to calculate and mark off enough metal to allow for bending and folding BECAUSE if such bending allowances are not made, the metal will not be sufficient for the bending and folding operations.

(i) Tin-plate, HOWEVER, should not be scratched too deeply.

or: HOWEVER, tin-plate should not be scratched too deeply.

(j) Tin-plate, however, should not be scratched too deeply SINCE the protective coating may be removed.

EXERCISE D *Restatements using expressions of time*

1. after   2. while   3. before   4. while   5. before   6. while   7. after.

EXERCISE E *Extracting information from the reading text*

Part 1

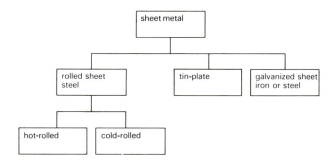

Part 2

MATERIAL	OPERATION
sheet metal	bending
mild steel	pressing
tin	cold-rolling
tin-plate	hot-rolling
galvanized iron or steel	plating
zinc	coating with zinc = galvanizing
	bending and folding
	marking out

EXERCISE F *Writing instructions for illustrations*

Part 1

(a) *How to use a file:*
   fit correct size handle on tang
   place workpiece securely in vice
   position vice at correct height
   place workpiece as low as possible in vice
   adopt correct stance
   keep file square with work
   press down evenly on file

(b) *How to dress correctly:*
   wear a one-piece overall of correct length
   fasten buttons
   roll up sleeves tightly
   wear safety boots, or shoes
   do not carry sharp tools in pockets
   do not wear rings or watches
   keep hair short or protected

(c) *How to chisel:*
 always direct chiselling away from body
 hold chisel firmly at angle of 30°–40° to cutting plane
 keep elbow of striking arm close to body
 direct eye to point of chisel
 wear goggles
 position chipping screen in front of work
(d) *How to hacksaw:*
 choose correct grade of blade for the job
 position work close to top of vice
 start work with blade sloping at angle of approximately 30° to cutting plane
 grip handle of hacksaw firmly in one hand
 hold forward end of frame in other hand
(e) *Before welding,* or, *safety measures for welding:*
 wear goggles to protect eyes
 wear gauntlets and leather apron
 make sure gas and air lines are in good condition
 check connections between torch and gas and air lines
 place screen in front of work
(f) *How to use a tap:*
 support workpiece securely in vice
 drill hole to tapping size of thread
 make sure tap is at 90° in all planes to the work
 turn tap backwards after every forward turn
 use cutting fluid

Part 2
(a) correct size handle fitted on tang
 workpiece securely placed in vice
 workpiece placed as low as possible in vice
 correct stance adopted
 file kept square with work
 press down evenly on file
(b) one-piece overall
 buttons fastened
 sleeves rolled up
 safety boots, or shoes
 no sharp tools
 no rings or watch
 hair kept short, or protected
(c) direct chiselling away from body
or: chiselling directed away from body
 elbow of striking arm close to body
 eye directed to point of chisel
 wear goggles
 chipping screen in front of work
(d) correct size blade chosen for job
 work close to top of vice
 blade sloping at 30° to cutting plane
 handle gripped firmly
 end of frame held in hand
(e) goggles
 gauntlets
 leather apron

> gas and air lines in good condition
> connection between torch and gas/air lines checked
> screen in front of work

(f) workpiece securely supported
> hole drilled to tapping size of thread

or: drill hole to tapping size of thread
> tap at 90° to work
> tap turned backwards after every forward turn
> use cutting fluid

or: cutting fluid used

EXERCISE G *Writing recommendations and rules*

①Part 1

(a) *How to hollow soft metal:* A sand bag should be placed on the work bench. The sheet of soft metal should be supported on the sand bag. A blocking mallet should be used to hollow the metal.

(b) *How to upset a mild steel bar:* The bar should be heated at the part to be upset. It should be held with tongs vertically on the anvil face. A sledgehammer should be used to increase the thickness of the bar.

(c) *How to cut a metal bar with a chisel:* The bar should be placed on the ledge of the anvil and held with open mouth tongs. A top chisel should be placed where the cut is to be made and struck with a sledgehammer.

(d) *How to thin down sheet metal:* Before hammering, the surface of the metal should be annealed and cleaned. The sheet metal should be placed on a block of wood supported in a vice. A planishing hammer should be used to thin down the metal.

(e) *How to keep the work bench tidy:* The bench should be kept free of waste material. Only the tools needed for the job should be on the bench. Tools should be returned to their proper places. The vice should be closed when it is not in use. Drawers should be kept tidy.

(f) *How to drill a hole:* The workpiece should be properly secured and there should be proper support for the break-through. The hole should be correctly marked out and centrepunched. The drill should be positioned directly above the hole and the guard should be in place before and during drilling.

(g) *How to anneal a work-hardened steel bar:* The bar should first be heated to dull red. Then, it should be allowed to cool slowly in sand, lime or ashes. Finally, it should be tested with a file. The metal should be soft enough to work easily.

①Part 2

The following from Exercise F are the best examples:
(b) A one-piece overall of the correct length must be worn. The buttons must be fastened and sleeves tightly rolled up. Safety boots, or shoes must be worn. Sharp tools must not be carried in the pockets. Rings and watches must not be worn either. Hair must be kept short or protected.
(e) Goggles must be worn to protect the eyes. Protective clothing in the form of gauntlets and a leather apron must be worn. Gas and air lines must be in good condition and the connection between the torch and the gas and air lines must be checked. A screen must be placed in front of the work.
The following from Exercise G may be chosen:
(a), (b), (c), (d), (e).

Part 3

The following are suggestions:
1. You must always use a hammer with the head firmly fixed on.

or: A hammer must always be used with the head firmly fixed on.
or: Never use a hammer with a loose head.
or: Always use a hammer with the head firmly fixed on.
or: Don't use a hammer with a loose head.
2. You must always drill a workpiece with clamps in position.
or: A workpiece must always be drilled with clamps in position.
or: Never drill a workpiece without clamps in position.
or: Always drill a workpiece with clamps in position.
or: You must always use a drill with the workpiece clamped in position.
3. You must always wear safety shoes.
or: Safety shoes must always be worn.
or: Always wear safety shoes.
or: Never go without safety shoes.

ⓘUNIT 7 GRAMMAR

1. The guard on a drilling machine *must be* in place before the machine is switched on.
2. Welding equipment *should be* carefully inspected for possible faults before it is used.
3. When the wing nut at one end of a hacksaw frame is tightened, the tension in the blade *will be* increased.
4. Angle bends *may be* made in sheet metal by hammering the metal in a vice.
5. Micrometers are precision instruments and therefore they *should be* treated very carefully.
or: . . . and therefore they *need to be* treated . . .
6. A hacksaw blade with 30 t.p.i. *should be* used to cut sheet metal.
7. While the end of a metal bar is being drawn down, it *should be* kept at a bright red heat.
8. A surface grinder *may be* used to produce a smooth surface on metal.
9. Where there is machinery with moving parts, sleeves *must be* tightly rolled up above the elbow.
10. After a mild steel bar has been forged or improperly heat treated, it *can be* restored to its normal condition by the normalizing process.
11. Hand tools which are not properly earthed *must not be* used.
12. Ties and scarves *must not be* worn in the workshop as they can get caught in moving machinery.
13. Equipment used in electric arc welding *must be* in good condition. Therefore it *should be* regularly inspected.
14. Before welding with oxy-acetylene equipment the flame *must be* adjusted correctly to obtain a good weld because too much oxygen *will* contaminate the weld.
15. Unless the correct forging temperature has been reached the metal *will not be* forged properly.
16. After annealing, a mild steel bar *will be* malleable.
17. Hand-operated bench shears *may be* used for the rough cutting of metal strips.
18. Safety shoes *must be* worn in the machine tool workshop.
19. A forge *should be* well ventilated as the fumes given off from a coke fire are poisonous.

UNIT 8 READING PASSAGES WITH COMPREHENSION QUESTIONS

PASSAGE I: SOLDERING AND BRAZING

EXERCISE A

(NOTE The line numbers refer to the lines in the text where the answers to the comprehension questions can be found.)

(a) Soft soldering takes place between 183°C and 327°C and silver soldering between 650°C and 800°C, whereas brazing is done at temperatures between 850°C and 1000°C. (Lines 6–10)

(b) Soft soldering is employed in electrical work (i) because solder is a good conductor, and (ii) because the strength of the joint is not of primary importance. (Lines 13–16)

(c) When the strength of the joint is important brazing is the operation that should be chosen. (Lines 19–21).

(d) The head of an electric soldering iron is heated by an internal element. (Lines 24–5)

(e) The high temperature of a brazing torch is obtained by mixing air or oxygen with acetylene gas. (Lines 28–9)

(f) It is known as an active flux because it both protects the surface of the metal and helps to clean it. (Lines 32–6).

(g) It is the low melting point of solder which makes it suitable for soldering work. (Line 45).

(h) Spelter can be made stronger by adding nickel to the alloy. (Lines 50–1).

EXERCISE B

(a) parent metals (2)
(b) joint faces (2)
(c) fusible alloy (1)
(d) filler metal (7)

(e) brazing hearth (12)
(f) working head (25)
(g) gas-air blow torch (27)

EXERCISE C

	FUSIBLE ALLOY	FLUX	APPLIANCE	TEMP. RANGE	USES
SOFT SOLDERING	common solder	rosin	soldering iron	183–327°C	electrical work
	plumber's solder	tallow	plain		joining lead pipes
	tinman's solder	gallipoli oil zinc chloride ammonium chloride	electric		joining sheet metal
SILVER SOLDERING	silver solder	borax	blow torch	650–800°C	soldering copper, steel or brass components
BRAZING	spelter	borax	blow torch	850–1000°C	joining steel and cast iron components

PASSAGE II: WELDING

EXERCISE A

(a) however

(b) generally

(c) as a result

(d) however

(e) thus

(f) consequently

EXERCISE B

(NOTE The line numbers refer to the lines in the text where the answers to the comprehension questions can be found.)

(a) Forge welding is the joining of metals by hammering them together at a white heat, whereas true welding is the joining of metals by fusion. (Lines 1–3)

(b) A welded joint is strong because the parent metals are melted together and allowed to solidify using a filler metal of the same composition as the parent metals. (Lines 4–6)

(c) Carburizing occurs when there is an excess of acetylene in the flame. (Lines 13–14)

(d) It is desirable to be able to adjust the composition of the flame for particular welding jobs because an oxidizing flame is necessary for welding brass and bronze, but a carburizing flame is necessary for welding stainless steel. (Lines 14–16)

(e) Two wrought iron parts can be forge welded by heating the shaped parts to the correct temperature and then hammering them together. (Lines 20–1)

(f) The temperature required for hammer welding is higher than that for ordinary forging. (Lines 22–3)

(g) White sparks can be seen at a temperature of about 1350°C, when the wrought iron is white hot. (Lines 23–5)

(h) Sand is used as a flux to clean the surface of the work in order to obtain a good weld. (Lines 26–9)

(i) It is necessary to remove the slag during welding operations because it is formed from the liquid flux and impurities in the metal. (Lines 29–31)

(j) Hammering moves outwards from the centre of the joint to force out the slag and leave the welded surfaces clean. (Lines 29–33)

EXERCISE C

(a) Soldering is a metal joining process in which a fusible alloy such as solder is bonded to the joint faces of the parent metals. (I. 1–2)

(b) Brazing is a metal joining process in which a fusible alloy such as spelter is bonded to the joint faces of the parent metals. (I. 1–2)

(c) Tinning is the process of cleaning the iron while it is hot, dipping it in a special flux and applying the solder. (I. 31–2)

or: Tinning is the process in which the iron is cleaned while it is hot, dipped in a special flux and solder applied.

(d) Pickling is the operation done after silver soldering in which the work is dipped in dilute sulphuric acid. (I. 52–4)

(e) Hammer welding is the operation of heating shaped parts of wrought iron or mild steel to the correct temperature and then hammering them together. (II. 20–2)

or: Hammer welding is the operation in which shaped parts of wrought iron or mild steel are heated to the correct temperature and then hammered together.

(f) Oxy-acetylene welding is a welding process in which oxygen and acetylene are mixed in the correct proportions to produce a flame as high as 3300°C in temperature. (II. 8–10)

(g) Solder is a fusible alloy which is made from tin and lead. (I. 1, 40–1)

(h) Spelter is a fusible alloy which is made from copper and zinc. (I. 1, 49–50)

(i) Fluxes are substances which either protect the metal surface that has been cleaned or both protect the surface and help to clean it. (I. 32–4)

(j) Slag is a substance which is formed from the liquid flux and impurities in the metal during hammer welding operations. (II. 29–31)

(k) A carburizing flame is a flame in which there is an excess of acetylene. (II. 13–16)

(l) An oxydizing flame is a flame in which there is an excess of oxygen. (II. 13–16)

PASSAGE III: MARKING OUT

EXERCISE A

(a) alternatively	(d) consequently
(b) for example	(e) also
(c) thus	(f) however

EXERCISE B

(NOTE The line numbers refer to the lines in the text where the answers to the comprehension questions can be found.)

(a) Two datum edges can be obtained by filing two adjacent edges straight at 90° to each other and to the face of the component. (Lines 8–10)

(b) A surface gauge may be used in marking-out operations when the work is placed perpendicular to the table top. (Lines 5–6)

(c) Copper sulphate is applied as a marking-out medium to the surface of a component before marking out. (Lines 12–14)

(d) The use of a marking-out medium such as copper sulphate assists the marking-out operation by making the scribed lines more clearly visible. (Lines 15–17)

(e) It is important that marking-out tools should be checked for sharpness because scribed lines should be as fine as possible so as to ensure the greatest degree of accuracy. (Lines 18–22)

(f) Witness dotting should be performed after marking out if the line is to be machined. (Lines 23–5)

(g) 'Boxing' helps to ensure accurate drilling by assisting the accurate positioning of the drill. (Lines 27–8)

(h) The flatness of the surface of a marking-out table is essential for accurate work because it provides a reference plane on which the work can stand. (Lines 32–4)

(i) The working face of a marking-out table can be smeared with oil to prevent rust forming. (Lines 34–7)

EXERCISE C

(a) A surface gauge is used for marking lines. (6)

(b) An angle plate is used for clamping the work to with toolmaker's clamps. (6–7)

(c) An engineer's square is used for checking angles. (10–11)

(d) Emery cloth is used for brightening the surface of the metal. (14–15)

(e) A prick punch is used for witness dotting lines that have been marked out with a scriber. (24–5)

(f) A centre punch is used for witness dotting lines that have been marked out with a scriber. (24–5)

(g) Copper sulphate is used *as* a marking out medium. (12–14)

EXERCISE D

(a) The *work* is laid flat on a marking-out table and the lines are scribed from two *datum edges* using a *try-square* (or engineer's square) and a scriber. The scriber should be *tilted slightly*.

(b) The work is placed perpendicular to the table top against an angle plate and scribed from two *datum edges* using a surface gauge.

PASSAGE IV: THE DRILLING MACHINE

EXERCISE A

Expressions from Diagram 1 to be inserted in the blank spaces in the text in **the** following order:
Base plate, belt housing, controls, operating lever, drill chuck, spindle, base plate, locking handle.
Expressions from the text to be inserted in Diagram 1:
(a) spindle (b) work table (c) work bench (d) motor housing (e) column

EXERCISE B

(NOTE The line numbers refer to the lines in the text where the answers to the comprehension questions can be found.)
(a) The electric motor drives the drill spindle by providing rotary motion which is transmitted to the drill spindle by the belt drive. (Lines 13–15)
(b) There is more than one set of pulleys so that the spindle speed can be changed by moving the drive belt to another set of pulleys. (Lines 15–16)
(c) The fitter can feel the drill cutting through the metal by lowering the drill into the work manually so its progress can be felt. (Lines 16–17)
(d) When the fitter releases the operating lever the spindle returns to its uppermost position. (Lines 18–19)
(e) A drill with parallel shanks must be used in a drill chuck. (Line 23)
(f) The jaws of the drill chuck are tightened with a chuck key which has a peg on the end which is inserted into one of the three holes on the chuck so that the jaws move uniformly in or out. (Lines 23–7)
(g) If the drill is loose in the drill chuck it will revolve in the jaws, and this will damage the drill. (Lines 27–9)

EXERCISE C

(a) a sensitive drilling machine (1)
(b) a cast iron base plate (Diagram 1)
(c) the belt drive (6)
(d) the belt housing (Diagram 1)
(e) the locking handle (Diagram 1)
(f) the feed pressure (18)
(g) the drill chuck (Diagram 1)

FURTHER COMPREHENSION EXERCISES

EXERCISE A

DESCRIPTION	REPORT
1. *The* faces of *the* iron *are* clean*ed* with *a* file or *with* emery cloth.	The faces of the iron *were* cleaned with a file or with emery cloth.
2. *The* iron *is* dip*ped* into *a* flux and tinn*ed* with solder.	The iron *was* dipped into a flux and tinned with solder.
3. *The* flux *is* appli*ed* to *the* metal surfaces *which are* to be joined and both surfaces tin*ned.*	The flux *was* applied to the metal surfaces which *were* to be joined and both surfaces tinned.
4. *The* two pieces of metal *are* clamp*ed* together.	The two pieces of metal *were* clamped together.
5. *A* clean hot iron *is* run over *the* surface of *the* joint so solder *is* evenly distributed along *the* joint.	A clean hot iron *was* run over the surface of the joint so solder *was* evenly distributed along the joint.

①EXERCISE B

(a)   *How a forge welded vee joint is made*

Two bars of black mild steel are taken and one end of one bar is heated to bright red, up to 35 mm. The end is upset on the anvil face up to 35 mm. The upset end is (then) reheated to bright red up to 50 mm. The bar is gripped in a vice and split with a hot set for about 35 mm down. (Next) one end of the second bar is upset to form a slight bulge. The first piece is reheated, opened and the second piece is inserted into it. (Then) the ends of both pieces are reheated to bright yellow. When the correct temperature is reached the ends are raised slightly above the fire and flux thrown on. (Then) the workpiece is replaced in the fire and raised to a white heat. (Finally) it is transferred to the anvil and the scale knocked off by holding each end with vee bit tongs and hammering from the centre outwards.

(b)   *How a forge welded vee joint was made*

(The same text as in (a) above using *past tense* verb forms. e.g. *were taken, was heated, was upset* etc.)

EXERCISE C

Part 1

The work hardened steel bar *was* heated to dull red and allowed to cool slowly in sand (or: *in ashes*) It *was* then tested with a file. It *was* found that the metal's malleability and ductility *was* restored, which *made* it workable again.
etc. changing the verb form to the past tense.

Part 2

The correct size of handle *was* fitted on the tang. The workpiece *was* placed securely in the vice which *was* positioned at the correct height. The workpiece *was* placed as low as possible in the vice to avoid vibration and screeching. The correct stance *was* adopted to maintain balance. The file *was* kept square with the work and both hands *were* pressed down evenly on the file.
etc. changing the verb form to the past tense.